Secrets
of
Personal Persuasion

Secrets
of
Personal
Persuasion

William Turner

Prentice-Hall, Inc.
Englewood Cliffs, New Jersey

Prentice-Hall International, Inc., *London*
Prentice-Hall of Australia, Pty. Ltd., *Sydney*
Prentice-Hall Canada, Inc., *Toronto*
Prentice-Hall of India Private Ltd., *New Delhi*
Prentice-Hall of Japan, Inc., *Tokyo*
Prentice-Hall of Southeast Asia Pte. Ltd., *Singapore*
Whitehall Books, Ltd., *Wellington, New Zealand*
Editora Prentice-Hall do Brasil, Ltda., *Rio de Janeiro*

Library of Congress Cataloging in Publication Data

Turner, William
 Secrets of personal persuasion.

 Includes index.
 1. Public speaking.   2. Persuasion (Rhetoric)
I. Title.
PN4121.T87 1985   808.5′1   84-17738

ISBN 0-13-798687-4

ISBN 0-13-798679-3 {PBK}

Printed in the United States of America

To Sally Stokes

...helpful
...competent
...deserving

Your Ticket to Success
in Any Speaking Situation

The power to persuade is the power to succeed.
Throughout all ages the ability to speak has been a
prerequisite for leadership. It is like a ladder pressing
firmly against the pinnacle of success. No matter what
rung you are currently on, as you ascend you will become a
greater achiever—a more effective performer in your
chosen field.

Men and women who have made impressions on
society were good speakers. Demosthenes, an ancient
Greek orator, said, "As a vessel is known by the sound,
whether it be cracked or not, so men are proved by their
speeches whether they be wise or foolish."

Moses, the great leader who directed the Jewish exodus from Egypt, was a faltering speaker. His brother,
Aaron, became Moses' stand-in communicator.

In American history the great social and political
influencers were competent pulpit clergymen, or political
leaders like Daniel Webster, Patrick Henry, James Madison,
and scores of others whose persuasive tongues and profound thoughts helped to forge a nation.

But we live here and now. Is persuasive speech still a
requisite for accomplishment in a computer-dominated
society? Don't ever doubt it. The succession of presidents
since Franklin D. Roosevelt have retained a staff of speech
writers and often have had specialists available to coach
them on delivery techniques.

For nearly twenty years, before becoming a full-time
speaker and writer, I helped dozens of executives in our

corporation to develop skills on the platform and in committee sessions. *Our society runs on communication.* More than ever it is important that civic and business leaders speak well. Every year, thousands of people flock to speaking seminars or hire private tutors to assist them.

You must realize that you, too, have need for special training because you have turned to this book for help. In it you will discover—and master—the techniques that will direct you to the top. The secrets of persuasion begin their work the moment you start to use them. They will show you how to reach a place of excellence on the public platform, in group discussion, in conversation, and in every other situation where you want your best to shine through. As you proceed through the secrets of persuasion, your boss, your associates, and even your family will see the improvement. *Clear expression, bubbling enthusiasm,* and *compelling results* will become power tools in your hands.

Many people, even those with years of experience, reach a plateau in their speech development and cease to climb. It happened to me and it has happened to many of my friends. Because we are exposed every day to a wide spectrum of professional talent—on television and on the speaking podium—mediocrity on the platform has become less and less satisfactory.

This book will boost you above the plateau of *so-so* speaking. You will learn how to develop a persuasive, conversational style, the kind of speaking tone readily accepted today. Specific, easy-to-understand secrets of delivery will be revealed:

How to use your voice properly.

How to add meaning and emphasis to your words with fluent body communication.

Practical steps for gaining attention.

Driving home your points and making a sale at the end.

How to find idea-support material and effective ways to organize it.

How to speak naturally without a script or even a handful of crippling notes. (That's right; soon you will be making thirty-minute speeches with no notes at all.)

As the secrets of persuasion unfold, you will gradually build greater confidence than you've ever known. This happens for three reasons:

1. You analyze the basis of fear and eliminate many of its causes, and you develop a proper attitude toward yourself.

2. You acquire skill in preparation so that nothing can go wrong.

3. You practice, practice, practice—in spare time, mind you—so that speaking becomes an enjoyable, easy experience.

As a bonus you will be given your own starter set of speech illustrations, quotations, and humorous stories. Good speakers have a reputation for using unique anecdotes that make their points easy to remember. Two chapters in this book are packed with excellent material and ideas for expanding and classifying your file. Your friends will soon begin to borrow from you, so be prepared to share or refuse.

Four other real benefits are in store for you:

1. Practice exercises, called *Skill Builders,* are provided in most chapters.

You won't need to wade through scores of hard-to-understand instructions. I've spent twenty years culling the superfluous and selecting methods that bring quick results. Breeze through them regularly, and soon the marks of excellence will radiate to your listeners.

2. The secrets of personal persuasion are applied to all phases of communication—conference, conversation, discussion, and the public platform.

I've heard colleagues and acquaintances say, "I'm comfortable in small conferences, but I crumble in front of a large crowd." Or conversely, "Big groups don't bother me, but I get tense in conversation."

There are obvious differences in various kinds of speaking, but you are going to learn universal techniques for handling all situations effectively. These techniques, blended with the confidence you acquire, will implant excellence in all of your engagements, from personal dialogue to the spotlighted lectern.

3. To help you advance at maximum speed, each chapter has a Magic Memory Stamp, a quick review of the highlights.

Each Memory Fixer is brief yet comprehensive. Most of them can be reviewed in only a few seconds. I suggest you do this often to reestablish the secrets of personal persuasion and to help you retain the continuity of the entire system.

4. *Success Secrets* are sprinkled generously throughout the book, each providing an additional secret to steer you to excellence. Repeat them often and memorize those that help you most.

This personal persuasion course will serve you for the remainder of your life. Its rewards will live on, creating for you one successful experience after another.

Furthermore, long after you have read the book and completed its Skill Builders, you'll want to return to it for refresher charges. You will restudy special portions that give you reinforcing help. Keep the book handy so you can repeat the Skill Builders that add professionalism to your personal persuasion. *Remember that the Skill Builders are stepping stones to success.*

By reading this far you have already demonstrated that you possess the essential ingredient of motivation: DESIRE. Whether you are a beginner with your foot on the first rung of the ladder, or an experienced speaker seeking to leave the plateau, be persistent. Prepare to join the parade of people who know where they are going and realize that personal persuasion will take them there.

As the great motivator, Zig Ziglar, often says, "I'll see you at the top."

William Turner

Contents

Contents

chapter 1

How to Penetrate the Audience Barrier

Many years ago I was a private pilot, one of those people frequently referred to as "weekend flyers." I shall always remember the first time I carried passengers. It was a scorching day in Minneapolis. On the taxiway at International Airport six aircraft waited ahead of me for takeoff clearance. With the cabin door swinging open to catch the cooling breeze, I inched my plane toward the runway.

Finally, I reached takeoff position, and the tower operator barked, "Yankee 6749, cleared for immediate takeoff!" My pulse raced as I locked the cabin door and opened the throttle in one continuous operation. The engine sputtered, then recovered, and soon we were roaring down the hot concrete. At the precise moment for liftoff I pulled back the wheel. Instead of rising, the airplane veered sharply to the left, reacting more like a tractor than a well-tuned flying machine. I lowered the nose to increase airspeed and then pulled the plane into a climbing position. As we ascended toward assigned altitude, I exhaled sharply. My passengers were alarmed. They never regained confidence, and *neither did I*. The more I brooded about the incident, the more tense I became, and the more awkwardly I performed at the controls.

What does all this have to do with persuasion? It can be said in one sentence: *The takeoff sets the tone for the entire speech.*

BEGIN WITH YOURSELF

Starting a speech or entering a conversation is like jumping into an icy lake. For many it's a fearful experience. For too many it's a deterrent to participation. But once the body is submerged, we realize that anticipation was worse than the plunge.

When you approach the lectern, remember that you must make a special kind of contact with the audience. Some call it unity, others call it rapport; but I call it *penetration*.

Regardless of the word, the objective is the same. You must reach out and touch the people, present your total personality: the face, the voice, the body action, and a positive psychological attitude.

Let's begin right now to learn how to establish a strong physical and mental impression. So many speakers, especially just before starting a speech, recite to themselves the following negatives:

I can't do it.

I'll blow it for sure.

My message is no good.

I look funny.

I call these negative thoughts "Little Nibblers" because they keep rising to bite at our self-esteem. They burrow into our minds making us feel incompetent at the most critical moments.

> **SUCCESS SECRET: Those who drag their self-image in the dirt cannot achieve the power of personal persuasion.**

Here are two examples of how little things can be blown completely out of proportion and be misread entirely to the detriment of the speaker.

Example one

Once when I traveled to Iowa for an important speech, I took only one suit with me, freshly cleaned and pressed, still in the cellophane wrapper. After checking in at my hotel I rested for awhile, then rose to prepare for the banquet. Just before leaving my room, I put on my suit jacket. How awful! The cleaner had torn off the top button. It was too late to make repairs, and the only alternative was to remove the bottom button as well and speak with the jacket open. As I ate dinner, thoughts of the buttonless jacket distressed me. They nearly destroyed me. *Everyone will notice it,* I thought. Fortunately, as I began to speak, I dismissed the matter. Afterwards, as I visited with a couple who had sat near the head table, I subtly described my calamity. "That's funny," the man said. "Until you mentioned it right now, I hadn't noticed."

Example two

At another banquet held on the opposite side of the continent, my eyes settled on a distinguished-looking gentleman in the audience who sat expressionless throughout my speech. As though drawn by a magnet, my eyes perpetually returned to stare into his impassive face. I didn't let this indifferent person spoil my speech, but I did let him unnerve me. The irony of it came out at the end of the program. When I finished speaking, this gentleman jumped to his feet and initiated a standing ovation.

How fruitless had been my concern in both cases! People are not sitting out there ready to pick you apart unless you invite them to do so by spotlighting your imperfections and exposing your Achilles' heel.

SUCCESS SECRET: Think like a professional. Cast positive thoughts on your subconscious mind.

As you stand facing your audience preparing to make the initial penetration, remember that it is you who has been asked to speak. All the people out there are waiting to hear *you.*

Make the most of the situation. No one wants you to fail. Believe this, because it's true. The audience comes to profit from what you have to say, and you should enjoy the privilege of responding to their needs.

BEHOLD YOUR AUDIENCE

Think of those people in front of you as men and women, and perhaps children, who have needs: the need for information, for inspiration, or for the relaxation that accompanies entertainment. They may even need someone to analyze a controversial subject.

You should identify these needs as you prepare your speech. The program chairperson or the organization's officers can help you. Ask them many questions. Be a good listener and take notes on what you hear.

Example

A purchasing association asked me to speak at its convention banquet. It would have been easy to appear with a stock, general speech and hope for the best, but I didn't do it that way. Instead, I managed to obtain an hour's time with the association's president and found out the group's greatest need. They wanted help in setting management goals, methods for reaching objectives in their jobs.

This became my target for penetration. I opened with a poem about a man who never converted his "dreams and schemes into reality." At once the audience reacted warmly, and I successfully launched my speech, entitled, "What You Do is Up to You."

To be effective, you must leave no barriers between you and the people who have assembled to hear you. That's why I use the word *penetration*. Climb through, around, or over the barriers!

No matter how diverse your interests or how far removed you are from the world of your audience, a way can be found to penetrate the group. Let them witness you as an authority, as one who has worthwhile ideas, as a speaker who can share a hearty laugh. Once you have entered their circle, you'll find you can secure whatever responses you desire: laughter, nods of approval, questions, participation.

> **SUCCESS SECRET: If you fail to penetrate the barrier between you and the audience, it will grow bigger. Get off to a sloppy start, and recovery is difficult, credibility is submerged, relaxation disappears.**

HOW TO MAKE THE PENETRATION

The penetration should accomplish five things:

1. Gaining attention: Be sure everyone is on board.
2. Establishing yourself as an authority: Command respect from your audience.
3. Naming the need: Make known the need, either specifically or by implication, that you intend to meet.
4. Relaxing the group and yourself: Make it clear that the time together will be enjoyable and profitable for everyone.
5. Leading to your subject: The movement must be clear and natural.

SUCCESS SECRET: Begin strongly, but don't be a steamroller.

Never intimidate people with a domineering, arrogant approach. Don't overwhelm your listeners with dramatic tones, exaggerated gestures, or rapid, staccato speech. Some speakers perform as though they were karate experts shouting their way into combat. Although the steamroller method may seem to capture people by toppling them over, it actually raises a barrier that impedes acceptance and deflects communication. Avoid this method: It doesn't penetrate; it merely dents.

At the other end of the spectrum, a hesitant, stammering start is equally bad, perhaps worse. Timid speakers who begin with an uncertain takeoff brand themselves as amateurs, and inept ones at that.

There is a happy medium. Square off with a friendly, open approach. Face the crowd and let your stance, your face, and your attitude telegraph, "I CAN." Once you transmit this tacit message you are ready to use the surefire penetrators that will scoot you into your topic with everyone flying comfortably, confident that you are taking them on an informative, enjoyable trip.

SEVEN EASY STEPS FOR PENETRATION

1. Open with a story. All the world loves a story. Anecdotes that add action, suspense, and a bit of humor will launch your speech successfully. You will actually feel the audience quiet down, all eyes riveted on your face.

But the story must relate to your speech. *Never drag it in by the heels.* Be sure that it serves as a natural springboard to the body of your speech. Many speakers stamp themselves as inept by telling stories that are totally unrelated to the subject being presented.

For some strange reason, chairpeople think they must tell a story about the speaker. Too often the speaker feels he must tell a story about the chairperson. Unbelievable fabrication is the frequent result! I once heard a speaker begin his speech with, "I want to tell a story about our chairman. He loves to hunt, and one day he was hunting zebras in Africa." At this point the bottom fell out of the speech for the chairman had never hunted anything but pheasants on his own farm.

Some speakers are clever and competent enough to lead the audience out of the real world for a moment, causing them to set aside their critical faculties and enjoy a walk through fantasy. Unless you have reached this stage of competence, don't attempt to do it.

SUCCESS SECRET: Don't tell some preposterous, unrelated tale.

2. Develop a warm, original greeting. Make it fascinating, sincere, and genuine. Don't bombard the audience with incredible, glib compliments or they'll quickly label you as a fake.

It is so easy to greet someone with a warm smile and an original sentence or two, but, oh, the errors that are committed! How often have you heard speakers begin with, "It gives me great pleasure..." Or, "I am deeply honored to speak to you tonight." The speaker may be sincere, but his takeoff is destroyed by trite, worn-out openers.

Here's another bummer: "Before I begin my speech, I want to tell you how honored I am..." In an effort to compliment his listeners, the speaker destroys himself. In the first place, what he is saying is not said *before* he begins his speech, it is *part* of his speech. In the second place, he is humbling himself before the audience, tarnishing his image in front of the very people he ought to be impressing.

Example

Years ago I took part in the American Legion Boys' State program in South Dakota. Each day's program was packed with speeches given by political dignitaries, most of whom arrived only a few minutes before they were introduced. By the end of the week-long program, the speakers were puzzled by the uproarious laughter that erupted as soon as they began to talk, although they were not attempting to be funny.

The reason was simple enough. Every speaker opened with the same remark: "I understand you boys are the cream of the crop." Although the boys' laughter was discourteous, it was an irrepressible response to what had become a ludicrous situation. One lad commented, "I wonder when we'll get churned."

SUCCESS SECRET: Outguess the other speakers. Develop creative openers that no one else has used.

3. Give your audience something physical to do. People like to be involved, even if it's only the simple act of raising the hand. Develop a mature, relevant exercise to fit the occasion. Have your audience follow a specific instruction, such as writing something on a notepad (perhaps some words you want to stress), or expressing an opinion by raising a hand to vote. There are many good audience-involvement activities you can devise.

SUCCESS SECRET: Involvement works wonders if you properly use its magic.

Three rules for physical involvement

a. Select a mature activity, not a kindergarten exercise.
b. Be sure the activity is relevant to the speech and that it leads to your subject.
c. Never select an activity that might embarrass anyone in the audience.

How it works

A friend of mine who is a professional speaker often discusses communication in leadership. After a short introductory statement, he commands his audience: "Follow me. Do what I do. Put your finger on your forehead." At the same time he touches his forehead near the hairline. "Now put your finger on your nose." He touches his own nose. His voice rises with excitement. "Now on your cheek," *but he touches his chin.* Most of the people invariably touch their chins also. No one is embarrassed as the speaker reprimands them for not having listened. His speech is launched. The audience is relaxed and ready to enjoy it, already convinced that they will learn about communication from this leader. (Obviously, this particular routine is soon borrowed by others and therefore becomes old stuff. Be creative. Invent fresh methods of your own.)

4. Begin with a strong quotation. An opening quotation can be a good penetrator. It need not be original, or even obscure. Indeed, well-known quotes have an advantage: Audiences warm to things they have heard before. Perhaps they experience a superior feeling because the words are familiar to them.

I once heard an excellent speaker urge his audience to cast off the crippling effects of failure. He opened by paraphrasing a quotation from James Barrie's play, *Dear Brutus:*

Three things do not come back: "...the spoken word,
the past life and the neglected opportunity."

—(Gearth's speech to Alice. Act I)

The audience became attentive immediately. The quotation was a natural platform from which the speaker launched his compelling theme. With a well-chosen tool he successfully penetrated the audience barrier.

5. Use a barrage of intriguing questions or startling facts. Too often this technique is overlooked by speakers, perhaps because they feel it's an unnatural way to begin. Not so; it can be natural and effective.

How it works

Face the audience for a moment, then unleash questions candidly and naturally, or burst on the scene with a series of thought-provoking, often alarming statements. Pull the trigger on your listener's minds. You can use this method whether you are presenting the annual message to corporate stockholders or charging your employees to adopt a positive attitude at work. The method works effectively in almost any situation. Let's take both these examples and demonstrate how they work.

Example 1: A report to stockholders

How much has high interest affected our earnings? How has government regulation stolen our management time? Did the merger with Imperial double our business potential? How can you help to make decisions in this corporation? Does our social responsibility program take earnings out of your pocket?

I'm positive your mind is seeking answers to these questions today, and answers to them you will receive.

Note: The speaker has not only caught attention (and penetrated the audience), he has also made a promise, which is an age-old technique for building interest.

The questions used above can be changed readily to direct, persuasive statements, that will launch the speech with equal success.

Example 2: To motivate employees

You can measure your personal effectiveness. You can work toward something day by day, or you can just work. You can plan each day, or you can merely let it happen. You can look at the record to see where you've been. You can take bearings on where you are and set the arrow towards where you are going.

Again, with questions and statements like these you have penetrated the barrier. By now, most people in the audience have been touched. By the nature of your challenging questions you have promised to help them reach their goals, advance their careers, and take charge of their lives.

6. *Develop a universal opening that can be adapted to what the chairman says or to things that happen at the meeting.* This technique may seem to be haphazard and risky, but it's not, although experienced speakers are likely to use it better than beginners. It does demand flexibility and confidence. Although the method may seem to be relying on the inspiration of the moment, it really isn't. It requires the ability to assemble existing material quickly and apply it to whatever occurs at the gathering. The choice is made from stories, jokes, descriptions, or explanations that refer directly to statements made or to happenings that preceded the speaker's appearance.

How it works

Example 1

I attended a meeting where the bachelor mayor of the host city delivered a welcoming address. Just before he began, he bent to kiss a beauty queen who was seated at the head table. The audience applauded and laughed. Somewhat embarrassed, the mayor began his remarks with, "It's all right for me to do that. After all, I *am* single."

A few moments later the main speaker was introduced. "Mr. Mayor," he opened, "your kissing Queen Marilyn was a warm, friendly act. But if I were to do that, I'd be single, too." The crowd exploded, the queen was flattered, the mayor was amused and the speaker launched with a successful penetration.

Example 2

I once traveled to Northwest Iowa with one of America's foremost speakers, Chris Christianson, for a speaking engagement. I am well-known in the area and prior to Chris' speech I was greeted by many old friends in the audience. Chris used my homecoming experience to penetrate his listeners. He talked about how people need each other, the value of affection, and the warmth of friendliness. It wasn't maudlin or corny: It was real, it was fresh, and it was effective.

To adapt to the situation at any given meeting I carry a list of quotations and illustrations that may fit many possible occurrences. The chairman's remarks or a unique incident that occurs at the meeting or banquet becomes a perfect setup for one of the stories or quotations in my file.

Example

At a cooperative association meeting, the president chided the members about making demands for more services when existing services were not being used. His comments, completely unoffensive, provided a perfect opening for the following anecdote from World War II days when sugar was tightly rationed:

A truck driver scooped several spoonfuls of the precious sweetener into his coffee before the waitress discreetly removed the sugar bowl. When she refilled his cup, the truck driver asked for more sugar. "What for?" the waitress asked. "You aren't stirring what you've got."

With a bit of practice, it's amazing how spontaneous you can be. Carry a few cards with key words that will help you to recall a story, or cards that contain short quotations, and you'll be able to adapt to nearly any kind of happening.

7. Refer to an event that's familiar to your audience. This technique is similar to the method described in number six. Talk about a local or national news event, a winning football team, a bank robbery, a new building in town, some commendable community effort, or perhaps some project your listeners are working on. For example, if you were to address the Chamber of Commerce, referring to local progress would be a superior technique. Be careful, however, not to bring up an unpopular event. Be sure that your approach actually penetrates and leads you gracefully to your subject.

> **SUCCESS SECRET: Never talk down or be condescending. It's a sign of a personal image that has climbed too high.**

I open my speeches with a radical method you might label corny. It may be, but it works so well for me that it's my trademark. I've used it in speeches made to a thousand listeners, as well as to small groups of only ten. When I'm introduced, I start my speech while still at the table, or occasionally from a remote position in the audience. Incidentally, I use a very small, cordless microphone whose mini-transmitter is concealed in my pocket. The audience is invariably surprised, but always intensely quiet. At an appropriate moment, without interruption (or ultra-dramatic activity) I rise from the table and face them. Often, I move into the crowd as I continue the opening. By this time, I'm "in their tent." I've penetrated the barrier.

> **SUCCESS SECRET: Dare to be different. Dare to do it your own personal way.**

Remember your goals: to join the audience in mutual respect, to be part of the bond that holds them together, to open a clear pathway to the subject of your speech.

A few final words. Don't rely on the inspiration of the moment. I acknowledge that some speakers do, with excellent results. They are either consistently inspired or invariably lucky. I strongly suspect that most are supplied with a deep reservoir of canned material and a strong ability to tap it. Their resourcefulness in fitting the material to the situation results in the appearance of *unrehearsed spontaneity*. (Go back and read technique six.) It's an effective method when you are ready to use it. Until you are, avoid the risk and carefully plan your opening. Ben Jonson, the English writer, once said, "Talking and eloquence are not the same: to speak, and to speak well, are two things. A fool may talk, but a wise man speaks" (*Discoveries Made upon Men and Matter*).

Begin with persuasive clout. Relaxed and ready, face your audience; listen to the silent voice inside you repeating, *"I'm ready. I can."* Then let your body do what you've trained it to do. You'll be amazed to discover that your audience relaxes as you relax. Become aware of this effect. It's called *the circular response* (CR). Whatever you telegraph to your listeners floats back in kind. You catch it and transmit it again. *CR can work for you, or it can work against you.* Transmit concern and tension; they return. Send out friendliness and relaxation; they come bounding back. Release an emotion—laughter, grief, sympathy, whatever it is—and it returns. It's like the man trying to throw away his boomerang, the crazy thing always comes back.

LET'S PRACTICE

Skill Builders

We are ready for some good, solid (but fun) speech practice. Select a topic from the following list (or make up one of your own). Pick something you are familiar with and something that interests you.

Suggested Topics

1. The American people are poorly informed on current events.

2. Camping is a great family activity.

3. The free enterprise system is being challenged today.

4. Our citizens aren't safe on America's streets.

5. Energy is everybody's business.

6. You can be what you want to be.

7. You can learn to speak in public.

8. Laughter is nature's best remedy.

Suggested Exercises (Practice one exercise each day)

1. On the first practice day, introduce your speech using the first method suggested in this chapter. Keep it brief, interesting, and motivating. Stand in front of the mirror, feet slightly separated with one foot two or three inches behind the other. Let your hands hang comfortably at your sides. Keep the body firm but not tense, relaxed but not flabby. As soon as you are comfortable, open your speech.

2. On the second practice day, use the second method, same topic. As you proceed through the methods, using a new one each day, notice how much easier it is for you to start your speech effectively.

3. On the eighth day, start all over using the same topic. On the second trip around you'll be impressed with your improvement. You'll feel comfortable. You'll know you are being effective!

PRESS THE MAGIC-MEMORY STAMP

Always prepare for the opening of your speech.

The first task is to gain attention.

To be effective you must penetrate the barrier to your audience and become part of their common bond.

Establish yourself as an authority.

Never intimidate. Don't talk down. Don't be a "steamroller."

Seven easy ways to begin:

1. Tell a story, a funny one if it's appropriate.
2. Develop an original greeting.
3. Give the audience a physical activity.
4. Use a strong quotation.
5. Use a barrage of intriguing questions or startling facts.
6. Develop a universal opening that can be adapted to most situations.
7. Refer to an event that's uppermost in everyone's mind.

Do things that are natural and comfortable to you, but ALWAYS REMEMBER WHY YOU ARE DOING THEM.

A LOOK AHEAD

Delivery is the heart of the persuasive process. It has many complex parts, but knowing what you will say and *programming* yourself to say it in proper order are probably the most important elements.

Some people believe that every word in a speech must be written down. They fear that they will falter in a speech or fail in a conference if they do not use a script. But there is a secret for speaking without notes, and in the next chapter, you will find out this secret. You will learn how to assimilate material, refine it, and fix it in your mind for replay. After you discover the technique and apply it a few times in practice, you will become amazed at how readily your ideas will march forth in a persuasive style.

Approach the task with confidence. The skills you acquire will carry over into every phase of personal communication from public speaking to social conversation.

chapter 2

Persuade with a Freewheeling Delivery

There is an old expression, "The proof of the pudding is in the taste." The proof of a speech is in the audience reaction. This chapter reveals how to *put it across*. You will master the tools of spontaneous personal persuasion in dialogue and in discourse.

Rise above the ordinary. Be extraordinary. Taste the joy of genuine communication. Free yourself from the binding slavery of a script. Acquire the three Cs of personal persuasion: *Confidence, Control,* and *Consistency*. When you find them, you will soon discover that excellence has its own reward; accomplishment is a super thrill.

In our electronic world, professional production has become a standard procedure. People have grown to expect a skilled performance. If they don't receive it, they'll tune you out. At a large national convention I attended, one of the speakers droned on for thirty minutes with eyes glued to his script. Throughout the vast auditorium, scores of persons slumped in their chairs, eyes closed, and, no doubt, brains in neutral. Some people whispered softly among themselves—and others whispered not so softly. The speaker's scholarly and important message either evaporated in the air or sounded like meaningless babble to nearly two thousand nonlisteners.

Then with a quick change of pace, the next speaker came along. Displaying minimum effort, he reassembled the crowd. His personal magnetism (something you also possess), radiated throughout the room, moving us easily from laughter to serious contemplation as he unfolded an impelling message. Frequently the audience punctuated his speech with enthusiastic applause. At the end, two thousand people rose as one body to deliver a deserved ovation.

When the session ended, I left the auditorium at once to record my impressions, purloin some of the speech material, and identify the differences between these two individuals. Although speaking on different topics, the level of difficulty was nearly equal for both men. Personality played a significant role. One man was dull; the other ebullient. The speaker who lulled us to sleep used few illustrations, only deadly prose. The second speaker presented lively examples containing real situations and real people, or at least he made them seem real.

But the major discernible difference between the two was the second speaker's freedom from a script. His sharply focused eyes moved from one area to another in the audience. His sentences sparkled. He was able to react immediately to silent messages that were telegraphed from the sea of faces in front of him.

Can you do it? Can you face your listeners without notes, fortified by the three Cs of communication?

Let's repeat them:

1. *Confidence*—in yourself, in your ability to create on your feet.

2. *Control*—over the situation. You determine what's going to happen and you see that it does.

3. *Consistency*—in every appearance. Discover that the system works and that you meet high standards of performance every time you appear on the platform.

I cannot make an absolute promise that you'll be able to toss aside your script or divorce yourself from all notes, but I have seen hundreds of speakers do it, some of them very unlikely prospects. I can show you how to do it and I can encourage you to try. Never forget this: Hundreds have mastered the techniques and have later said, "Thanks for opening the door to personal persuasion."

As you continue your development, keep in mind that this chapter rests on the assumption that you can—and will—reduce your notes to a minimum, while still retaining the important elements of clear communication: unity, coherence, meaning, and emphasis. But first let's look at some of the more constricting methods of delivery.

AVOID THE HAZARDS OF MEMORIZED SPEECHES

I'm often asked, "Is it all right to memorize my speeches?" I'm quick to respond, "No!" Memorization has deadly pitfalls.

In the bygone years of polished rhetoric, students "learned their orations" to develop skill in body and vocal delivery. Speakers—and teachers, too—also emphasized writing skills, encouraging the use of carefully drawn words and sculptured sentences. Possibly the technique was rewarding, although the same amount of effort directed toward extemporaneous delivery might have achieved even greater results. Right or wrong, we have abandoned the pompous, stilted language of yesterday's speaking.

I acknowledge that memorizing the speech will free you from your script. I concede that it allows you to fix your eyes on the audience, practice gestures, and learn to intone sentences perfectly with meaning and feeling. BUT this may also lead to your becoming a parrot, mouthing words and mechanically swinging your arms because you "practiced it that way."

SUCCESS SECRET: Memorized speeches usually sound like memorized speeches.

Memory work, or even speaking from a script, is a gross misuse of time, particularly if you deliver the talk only once. There are other problems as well.

1. The speaker has no flexibility. He cannot adapt to happenings at the meeting.
2. The speaker is usually time bound. He can neither shorten nor lengthen his address. He must give it as he learned it.
3. If the speaker does become brave and ad-lib, the contrast is alarmingly apparent. All pretense of polish disappears.
4. If the speech is repeated several times, sincerity and spontaneity usually disappear. Only the most competent public speakers can make the material seem fresh after it has been through the mill more than two or three times.
5. And this horrible thought: *What if the speaker forgets his lines part of the way through!*

SUCCESS SECRET: The sincerity of a memorized speech is inversely related to the number of times it is repeated.

WHEN A PERSON NEEDS A SCRIPT

There comes a time when you absolutely must speak from a script. Perhaps accuracy demands it, complexity of the material demands it, or the boss demands it. It's entirely possible that you may have need to prove infallibly what you actually said at a meeting. Don't try to fight this circumstance. Instead, learn to use a script creatively and effectively.

For a moment, let us pursue the negative vein.

1. Script glues you to the lectern and tends to fasten your head in a slant/read position.
2. Unless you can ad-lib cleverly, you cannot adapt to events and to happenings at the meeting; or if you try to ad-lib,

you run into the same risk as in the memorized speaking situation. The contrast is usually alarming and damaging.

If circumstances or people require that you use a script, write one that is packed with personal persuasion. It can be done. Avoid a stilted, formal style. Try instead to sound conversational by choosing common words and assembling them in sentences that sound like normal, everyday speech.

Some suggestions:

1. Write in rhythmic sentences that are direct, preferably in the active voice. "The man struck the boy," is much better than, "The boy was struck by the man."

2. Keep your sentences short so you will be readily understood.

3. Use lots of examples, illustrations, and stories. Blend them in naturally, phrasing them as if you were telling a story at some social occasion.

4. If you must ad-lib, keep the contrasting style as un-noticeable as possible. You can learn to do this by writing the way you talk. You never can learn to talk the way you write.

5. Finally, practice, practice, and practice the script. Make it sound like you.

Speakers who deliver from the written page often need to practice more than those who seem to speak off the cuff. I'm not referring to the "word mill" who rambles and roams about *ad boredom.* I mean the creative, well-trained, and well-disciplined speaker who unfolds his interesting ideas persuasively without notes, or who has curtailed his note inventory to mere memory joggers.

SUCCESS SECRET. If you've got to read it, read it well.

How to deliver the manuscript speech:

1. If it helps, underline key words and key points.
2. Be intimate with every page.
3. Unclip the sheets so you don't make a lot of noise struggling from one page to the next.
4. While reading a specific page, slide it down slightly to uncover the top of the next one. This permits you to switch smoothly from the sheet you are reading to the one beneath it.
5. Practice, practice, practice!

SUCCESS SECRET: Extra effort will help you make script reading simulate extemporaneous delivery.

AD-LIB YOUR WAY TO PERSONAL PERSUASION

No speaker is more impressive than one who is competent, footloose, and free from copious notes or a rigid script. There is nothing more persuasive than a fluent participant in a meeting who "speaks his piece" effectively. Spontaneity enhances the magic power of personal persuasion. It lets you radiate a bit of yourself as you share a message with your listeners.

This power can be yours. You can learn it systematically and completely. The prerequisites are self-discipline, courage, and confidence. *This is a journey whose destination is excellence.*

SUCCESS SECRET: You need not write down every word. Train your brain to tell your mouth the things to say.

Extemporaneous speaking is a process that eliminates a time-consuming, crippling step without affecting the quality of your expression. To ad-lib your way through any presentation, your brain must be in gear. You must be hyperalert. You concentrate with pinpoint sharpness. In contrast, the script reader operates like a machine: his eyes slowly traverse each line, and his mouth transmits a steady, droning procession of words. I have often suspected that readers like this are not even aware of what they are saying.

But if you are up there alone without a script or notes—or with a minimum number of prompters or "prompt" words—your brain is actively processing your material. Every exciting idea is like a genie waiting to spring from its bottle. Your eyes sparkle as they focus sharply on people you expect to persuade. And, best of all, you can adjust to the situation, by shortening or lengthening your remarks, referring to the chairman's remarks, or bolstering a point with additional material because your brain is in charge and your brain knows what to do.

HOW TO PERSUADE WITHOUT A SCRIPT

The time has come to capture the power of ad-lib speaking. Everything begins with the preparation step. Work and rework your material until it actually becomes part of you.

When I was learning to fly, my instructor taught me to think of the aircraft as an extension of my body attached at the seat. This concept helped me learn to bank, climb, and land. I no longer maneuvered the plane: *I maneuvered myself.*

> **SUCCESS SECRET: If the speech is part of you, you cease to strain for the thoughts. They flow freely from the mind, and your body joins in to create a concert of delivery.**

I stress this magic point: The more frequently you process your material, the easier the delivery will be, whether it's informal participation at a meeting or a full-length address at a convention banquet.

Everyone must develop his or her own speech construction technique. Whatever works well for you is the proper system. I'm going to share mine. Use it if you can or adapt it to suit your needs.

I use a sequence of preparatory worksheets. As I create a new one, I throw the old one away. Each new sheet is a further refinement, a step closer to the final product. My starting point is to take a sheet of paper and write down the subject on which I plan to speak, not necessarily the title, (I frequently develop an appealing title after the speech has been completely prepared.) Then I write down everything I can think of about my subject: illustrations, anecdotes, quotations—whatever occurs to me. I write only a key word or phrase about each item, just enough to help me recall it.

Do you have enough material? If not, visit with other people. You'll soon discover that your friends and acquaintances provide many ideas that you can use in your speech. Reading is also a good source of information. Specialized books, encyclopedias, almanacs, and magazine articles are a bottomless well of supplementary support material.

In a later chapter, you will learn how to develop your own speech file. Because I collect material constantly, the task of speech preparation is largely one of selection rather than search.

SUCCESS SECRET: Speech ideas are everywhere. Make it a habit to collect them.

Now let's return to the sheet of paper. From now on the processes are incubation and assimilation. Classify your material. You will soon notice that items on the list fit into neat compartments, probably three major ones. These are the main points of your talk. As you classify these items, isolate the ones that are particularly suited for the introduction—real barrier penetrators. Other items may be excellent for your conclusion.

Your next sheet of paper is used for further refinement. Recopy the items under their various headings.

1. Barrier penetrators
2. Point one
3. Point two
4. Point three
5. Conclusion

Next create a persuasive statement for each point and rearrange the ideas under it so that the material provides strong, persuasive support.

> **SUCCESS SECRET: The more often you work with your material, the easier it will be to ad-lib your speech.**

Look over your outline again. See if there is enough material to make each point believable. Can you persuade with what you have? If not, round up more stories, more statistics, more quotations. Add reasons why people should believe what you are saying. Perhaps you have more material than you really need. Be sure that every item adds to the persuasion process. If something doesn't fit, discard it. If it can't be shaped to do its part, don't drag it in just because you like it.

When you are thoroughly satisfied that the material flows the way you want it to, you are ready to build in the memory devices that will help you speak without notes. For example, one of my speeches has four points. I use four "prompt" words to help me recall them:

1. Simmer
2. Launch
3. Impact
4. Milestones

Each of these words suggests one of the points in the speech. As an additional memory device, I purposely choose "prompt" words whose first letters form an acronym. In the example above, the word is *slim*. Although I did not foresee an additional use when I developed this system, a supplementary benefit to personal persuasion quickly evolved. Often I ask the audience to write down the acronym and follow along with me as I develop it. Occasionally, I even find it helpful as I finish a point to ask the audience for the next letter. A host of volunteers invariably chimes in.

> **SUCCESS SECRET: Audience participation is a strong factor in personal persuasion.**

It is most beneficial if you recopy your speech outline every day for about a week. Each time you go through it, the arrangement seems to improve. You may even find better words or more memorable phrases for your prompters. But more important, the mind captures the flow, selects words, and records the arrangement of material. In short, the mind is preparing to deliver the speech. Try to recall ideas; don't memorize words.

> **SUCCESS SECRET: If given rein, the mind can process material with great efficiency.**

USE THE MAGIC-PERSUASION PRÉCIS

To test your level of preparation, see if you can digest the meaning of your speech (its message) in about one hundred to one hundred-fifty words. Ask yourself this question (filling in your name where I have left a blank): All right, ____, what are you going to talk about?

Now answer the question by giving a very short résumé of your speech beginning with the introduction and ending with the conclusion. You'll find with a bit of practice that you can readily capture the theme, the flow, and the content of your entire speech and that it is a "programming step" for that great computer inside your head.

Use the Back of Abe's Envelope

Abe Lincoln was supposed to have written the Gettysburg Address on the back of an old envelope. Whether that is history or legend is immaterial. We can learn from Lincoln's ability to choose words carefully, arrange them with impact, and make each one work toward personal persuasion.

A few hours before your speech, find a place where you can be alone and write a short version of your outline. Fold a sheet of paper in thirds and reduce the abbreviated concepts to one panel. When you have acquired maximum brevity, you will realize that one word can bring to mind an entire paragraph, or even more.

Now, turn over your workpaper so you can't see the panel on which you have written. Try to reproduce this outline from memory. Use your "prompt" words and your acronym to help you to remember. When you have gone this far, you should be able to ad-lib your speech with total comfort.

Stick with the Material That You Have Planned

Resist the temptation to add ideas that suddenly pop into your mind while you are speaking. Green pastures often tempt the ad-lib speaker, and self-discipline is the antidote. If you do go astray, be prepared for two indictments: (1) a badly organized speech, and (2) a speech that goes beyond all time restrictions placed upon you.

> **SUCCESS SECRET: Your speech can be immortal without being eternal.**

AD-LIB SPEAKING LEADS YOU TO PERSUASIVE SUCCESS

Here are the advantages of speaking without notes.

1. You are free of the lectern. No more will you be shackled to a script.
2. You can shorten or lengthen your speech, adjusting to what happens at the meeting.
3. You avoid dullness and you construct a warm, circular response between you and your audience.
4. You understand thoroughly what you are saying. When *you* believe, your audience is persuaded.
5. The magic of accomplishment is learning to depend on yourself rather than on your script.
6. You will learn to package your speech attractively. Good packages do not ensure good products, but good products invariably have good packages. A bit of cellophane makes ordinary cheese look elegant and delicious.
7. Your eyes are free to look at people. Your mouth is projecting words into the crowd instead of bouncing off the hard surface of the speaker's stand.

PUT UP THE ROAD SIGNS OF PERSUASION

We have all driven along a dark highway on a rainy night and at times were able to stay on the road only by following the white stripes painted along the shoulder or down the middle. Have you ever thought how difficult it would be to find your way if the stripes were not there, or if there weren't signs along the roadside warning you of the curves and intersections ahead?

Speeches are a lot like that. Put up the signs. Use a good thread to tie together the segments of your talk. If you are changing from one idea to another, or from one point to another, let the audience know that you are making this alteration. Tell your listeners what you plan to do. Close out one thought with an appropriate summary or other concluding statement; then introduce the next. Never leave your listeners wondering where you are.

Examples

1. Announce your intention. "Let's move from last year's record and forecast tomorrow's."

2. Summarize what you've said and lead into your next point. "You've seen what people did in the past to make America great. Let's examine our contemporary record."

3. If your points are on the blackboard, draw a line through one of them to show that you have completed it. Then say, "Now let's look at the next step we are going to take."

4. Learn to use transition words that show relationships: *meanwhile, when, on the other hand, in contrast, then, next.* The list is infinite.

Never leave your listeners behind. Put up the signs that warn them when you are going to make a turn.

SUCCESS SECRET: Let the skeleton of your outline show. It's better that way than to have a glob of unorganized fat.

LET'S PRACTICE

Skill Builders

1. Find a copy of someone else's speech or a well-written magazine article. Highlight or underline the main

points. Stand up and read one page of the article aloud every day for a week. As you read, imagine that you are directing your message to a large audience.

2. Write down three sentences, each describing a familiar topic. On days one, two, three, and four, stand in front of a mirror (preferably full length) and talk about the first sentence you have written. (Do not use any notes.) State the sentence, tell a story about it, make up statistics if you need to, make up a quotation if you need to—just keep talking as long as you can. Talk naturally, persuasively, and make it a real speaking situation. Be as comfortable as possible in this easy-flowing talkathon. On the fifth day, practice the second sentence in the same way. Repeat for three more days. Finally on the ninth day, begin working on the third sentence. Practice this exercise at every opportunity, using every kind of support you can—statistics, quotations, explanations, humor—whatever you can think of.

PRESS THE MAGIC-MEMORY STAMP

Personal persuasion is easy with a direct approach to the audience.

Memorized speeches have few practical uses on the modern platform.

Although scripts must be used occasionally, they constrict the speaker.

If you must use a script, learn to use it well. Be familiar with it. Mark it so that main ideas will stand out. Be as direct as possible; read it in a conversational style.

Ad-lib speech is the most persuasive kind of speech.

Collect your speech material carefully. Arrange it and rearrange it as many times as necessary.

Reduce your final outline to the fewest possible number of words.

Use "prompt" words to aid the memory process.

Don't be enticed into green pastures as you deliver the speech. Stay with what you prepared.

Put up road signs so that your audience doesn't lag behind or fail to follow you.

A LOOK AHEAD

Ending the speech might seem easy, but it is not. A good landing requires skill, precision, and good planning. The next chapter will show you the following:

1. How to quit on a positive note.

2. How to go on persuading right through the last second of your speech.

3. How to "make the sale" with your audience.

You will discover nine secrets for ending a speech, and the Skill Builders will help you choose and use each one properly. Let's proceed to the next step in personal persuasion.

chapter 3

Land Your Speech with Persuasive Ease

One day I stood on an airport ramp anxiously watching a student pilot who was trying to land her plane. Once, twice, three times the young woman approached the runway. On each attempt she changed her mind, opened the throttle, and circled the field again. Finally, on the fourth descent the wheels smacked against the pavement, and the aircraft taxied safely to the hangar.

After encouraging their listeners to believe that the end is in sight ("and in conclusion, my friends..."), many speakers float away once more, attached to the tail of a fresh, new idea.

In Chapter 1 you learned how to penetrate the audience barrier. By now you have mastered the techniques. You are ready now to attack that important part of speech called the *conclusion*. You'll learn how to land your speech with magic ease.

Let's return to the airplane analogy for another moment. Even if you never had flying lessons, you probably know that landing is the most difficult skill to master. The altitude of the aircraft must be critically positioned; the airspeed and rate of descent must be exact. At a precise moment in the landing process, the plane must be stalled over the runway to let the wheels touch down gently. The instant and the position of that stall determine the difference between a landing and a crash.

From the moment your speech is launched, you are traveling toward a specific destination, a defined accomplishment. Although the audience may not be aware of it (and probably shouldn't be), your intensity increases as your speech moves onward. Confidence, fed by audience response, enhances your eloquence. The speech is under control. The airport is at close hand. *Don't spoil this effect.* Fire that final, climactic blow; then *land your speech with magic ease.*

AVOID AN UNPLANNED CLOSING

Unplanned closings lead speakers into undesirable practices. The last persuasive impression, perhaps the strongest, usually occurs in the final two minutes of your speech. To reach maximum power, here are some situations you must avoid:

1. Trailaway endings. When unable to find a suitable closing point, some speakers tack on a host of totally unrelated materials—stories, quotations, and factual statements—perhaps left over from the preparation process or from some other speech. This practice merely confuses the audience, destroys the unity of your speech, and detracts from your persuasive theme.

2. New-idea endings. There is an ironclad rule that the main points of a speech belong in the body of the speech and nowhere else. Speakers frequently try to close a speech by injecting a fresh idea or the embryo of a main point. Usually it is done at high speed with demolition potential.

Here's a true example from the public platform. I once heard a professional speaker, a man with a national reputation, lead his audience through a spellbinding hour on management principles. He realized that his allotted time was expiring. He was in the landing pattern. Then suddenly, like a two-minute drill in football, he injected a hasty, staccato discussion on goal setting, apologized for his speed, and then sat down, spoiling the effect of his speech. Afterwards, all we could really recall of this magnificent speech was its rushed and clumsy ending.

3. Chopped-off endings. Audiences like forewarning, especially if they are listening intently. Don't shock them with a chopped-off conclusion. The fault is usually in preparation. It's like making a sandwich with only one slice of bread: The opening is there, the meat is there, but the ending—the second piece of bread—has been omitted. Not only are the listeners caught unaware, but more important, the speaker reduces his persuasive power by failing to drive home his message with a strong conclusion.

4. Endless-promise endings. Lack of preparation is not usually the reason why many speakers go on and on. Rather, it's lack of discipline and failure to respect their time restrictions. It is true that the clock should condition preparation efforts, but a speech can be superior—well-prepared with loving care—and still be far too long.

For a moment, imagine yourself behind the lectern in this situation: With an allotment of thirty minutes on the program, you have already spoken for twenty-five, and you have at least ten minutes of material left. You realize that your listeners are edgy (and your meeting-planners, too) *even though you still have them in control.* What are your options? You have only one: *Terminate as soon as you can.* Gracefully slide around the remainder of the speech, get into the landing pattern, and set it on the runway.

But if you are typical, you may not follow this advice. Instead you will slip in that overworked expression, "In conclusion..." The faces in front of you will glow, their bodies will relax. But you are only fooling them. You aren't ready to stop, and soon they will realize it. Tension grows, so you try it again: "In conclusion..." I've heard it used as many as five times in one speech. The speaker who did it spoiled the effect of his entire speech and his credibility as well, even though his conclusion, when he finally reached it, was excellent.

Although I said earlier that lack of preparation does not cause endlessness, in a technical sense this is not true. Time allotment must always be a consideration when you are preparing. A speech perfectly sculptured and professionally delivered can still be destroyed by three simple words, "And in conclusion..."

> **SUCCESS SECRET: No one has ever been angry with a speaker for stopping five minutes early.**

NINE WAYS TO END EFFECTIVELY

Throughout the speech, what reactions have you sought from your listeners? What facts have you asked them to believe? Write these facts down, even before you begin your speech. I usually list them on top of my final outline. Go back to Chapter 2 and refresh your memory. In two or three crisp sentences, I state the main things I want from my listeners, the facts I want to persuade them to believe. What better place than in the conclusion to reinforce these points? Whatever you want from your audience, now is the time to ask for it. Let's learn to deliver that power punch. Here are nine magic ways to do it:

1. Ask for action or belief. To the salesman this is referred to as "calling for the order," one of the most important parts of the selling process. It is the ultimate measure of effectiveness. Think of yourself as a salesman. In that role, as you finish your address, ask your listeners to do whatever it was you set out to accomplish in your speech—vote, buy, write, cooperate, and so forth. Make your appeal and ask for it now. To fail in this step of the speech is to default in the entire mission. You must do it well to accomplish your persuasive result.

Example

A chief executive exhorted his staff to curtail expenses in the corporate budget. His reasons were valid and impelling. He gave case study examples of other corporations that had reached the brink of collapse because they failed to hold the reins on their administrative costs. The executive painted a bleak picture of dangers that lay immediately ahead on the financial highway. At this moment, nearing the end of his presentation, the speaker is ready to strike a telling blow. His success rests on the strength of that blow. With receptive minds, his listeners are waiting for him to tell them what their personal responsibilities are. *What must they do? When? How?* (The speaker has already told them *why* the company is in danger.) Now, *he must call for the order.*

The ending of a speech is comparatively simple to prepare when one analyzes it. The need for persuasive strength is apparent. Describe the specific action that you want. Whenever possible, promise to meet a human want: health, wealth, happiness, recognition, security, and the like.

In the instance above, the executive ended his speech like this:

Everyone in this auditorium has invested his life with our company. Your futures may well be at stake this year. Your salaries, your bonuses, your ultimate pensions can go up with the company's prosperity or go down with its failure. Within the next two weeks, you are to rework your budgets. I want you to slash them wherever they can be safely cut. No amount is too small to be overlooked. If you don't need something, don't plan to buy it. If you need something, see if you can delay its purchase until better times. Two weeks from today we shall return to this room where we will assess the results of your work. Plan, appraise, slash, until you reach your goal!

Notice that this executive appealed to the monetary side of his employees' needs. He could have asked for their cooperation on the basis of company loyalty. He probably was justified in using a veiled threat of monetary penalty for failure to reduce costs, but he carefully listed the action he sought from each individual.

The words I've given above are a paraphrase of the actual speech, but the situation was real. The action appeal netted a 17 percent reduction in general and administrative expenses for that company. The speech receives a rating of ten on a scale of ten for effectiveness.

> **SUCCESS SECRET: Thousands of orders are lost because the salesman forgets to ask for the order. Thousands of speeches miss their mark because speakers fail to ask for action.**

2. Wrap it up with humor. You may never have considered humor as a possible way to terminate a speech. More often it is a tool of the comic to "leave 'em laughing." Nevertheless, in specialized situations a bit of irony, a humorous incident, or a funny story can be a very effective way to end a speech, especially when you are seeking credibility or belief rather than overt action.

Here is an example: A speaker addressing an audience of farmers in New York State used humor very effectively. Throughout his address he kept pounding away at the premise that farmers' opinions should be solicited by America's political leaders. He ended with this story:

> A small Nebraska community could not afford a full-time trash hauler, so the city council advertised for someone with a truck to pick up garbage once a week. Art Rasmussen, a farmer, and his son, Henry, were accepted for the job. On the first day's pickup, a thirty-mile-an-hour wind was blowing from the north. As Art and Henry slowly filled the truck, newspapers, tin cans, and trash blew off and littered the community.

The city fathers, smarting from citizens' complaints, warned the Rasmussens that they must procure a tarpaulin for their truck. But Art couldn't find one prior to the next week's pickup, which turned out to be another windy day. As the truck box began to fill, Art said to his son, "We can't let 'er blow again this week, Son. Why don't you climb on top of that garbage and spread out to hold 'er down?" Slowly, Art drove the truck down Main Street with Henry lying on top of the load, his arms and legs spread out to keep it from blowing away. Just then, two salesmen came out of a restaurant. "Look at that, Mark," one of the salesmen said. "They are throwing away a perfectly good farmer."

3. Use a dramatic incident. This is one of the most powerful techniques available for ending your speech. If the incident is properly selected and expertly related, the message will be memorable. Your file of support material becomes invaluable for you at this moment. From it you should be able to find a story that is strong enough to deliver the punch and dramatic enough to make your message live on.

The example I have selected to illustrate a dramatic closing is obsolete by modern standards, but in its day it was a gripping story. I heard it delivered before a college audience in the pre-World War II era.

The speaker, condemning racial unfairness, made a twenty-minute appeal to end prejudice in colleges and universities. Although it was not a modern speech, it was well-reasoned, well-supported, practical. The speaker frequently repeated his thesis: *Prejudice is built on ignorance. Under proper conditions, prejudice fades and then disappears like magic.* To end his presentation, the speaker narrated the story of Franklin Alexander. I shall recreate that story as an example of how to use a dramatic incident as a climactic ending to a speech. After forty intervening years, I have never forgotten this gripping tale, although I must obviously paraphrase it at this time. Remember the theme of the message and the era in which the speech was given. Here is the story:

> A college speech fraternity scheduled its annual foren-sic contest in the deep South. In that era, civil rights were for white folks only. During his two-year college career, Franklin Alexander, a black man, had become a superior orator. In the northern college where he was a student, race had not been a deterrent to his success. Perhaps with misgivings, or perhaps thoughtlessly, the speech director entered Franklin Alexander in the national event. But the host school would not let him compete in the traditional manner. During the first round, the judges listened to other contestants, then adjourned to a black Baptist church where Franklin Alexander was permitted to speak. Alexander won first place. In the second round, the black man also led the pack—and in the third, and in the fourth. The final contest was a grand finale held before a large crowd in the college auditorium. One after another four finalists addressed the group, and then the fifth was introduced—Franklin Alexander. A concerned muttering rippled through the crowd as a tall, handsome black man walked onto the platform and began to speak in deep, sincere tones. An immedi-ate hush fell over the crowd. For ten minutes, as though hypnotized, the listeners were awe-inspired by the man's message. The spell lingered for a long silent moment even after Alexander had finished talking. Suddenly wild applause exploded in the arena and increased to an ascending roar. Then two and three at a time, people jumped to their feet, clapping wildly. Others quickly joined them until soon the entire audience stood en masse to deliver a thunderous ovation. Prejudice rises from ignorance. Under proper conditions, prejudice fades and disappears as we place our judgments where they rightly belong.

Thus a speaker successfully used a dramatic incident to end his speech. He too received a standing ovation. His point was driven home effectively, memorably, and persuasively.

4. Close with an illustration, a poem, or an appropriate quotation. Obviously these elements are very similar to the dramatic incident described above. Success in using them depends on three conditions:

a. *Make the proper selection.* Chris Christianson, a premier American platform personality, likes to end his powerful addresses with persuasive and very appropriate pieces of verse. His success lies in the infinite variety of poems he has committed to memory. He is a reciter with a verse for every speaking occasion. Pick the proper story, poem, or quotation. Always keep the speech file open.

> **SUCCESS SECRET: Continue to fill your speech file with the best material you can find. Paste a label on your box or notebook that reads, "The Speaker's Magic Friend."**

b. *Deliver your closing illustration with sincere feeling.* Be persuasive. Be powerful. Let the words reach out and grasp your audience. Send the listeners out of the meeting with that closing story burning inside them. When you are able to accomplish this consistently and repeatedly, you will have truly mastered the magic power of personal persuasion.

c. *Tie the closing element tightly to the message itself.* Sometimes the story, quotation, or poem is such an accurate miniature of your entire theme that an additional tie-in can be eliminated, or at least held to a minimum. A rule of thumb: the more appropriate the closing element, the less glue you need to attach it. Spend time meditating on this question: *What are the best possible ways to tie it all together?* The answers will direct you toward a good transition to the ending element. They will tell you whether you should tack on a final closing statement or whether you should terminate as soon as you have delivered the closing element. Pick the method that seems the most persuasive. If you deliver the speech several times, experiment with other options and mentally record listener reactions. Not only will this enable you to end the speech in the most effective manner, but it will also give you good practice in developing a variety of techniques.

5. Use personal commitment to close the speech. Audiences are always impressed when a speaker offers his own personal pledge to "march in the parade," "ring doorbells," "be an example," or "seek other recruits."

This kind of dedication was captured by Norman Rockwell in his picture of a laborer addressing a group of entranced listeners. I always imagined that the man was finishing his speech by declaring his belief in the union's cause. I've heard speakers conclude their message with a ring of strength and power by merely proclaiming their own stand. The best-known example came from the fiery mouth of Patrick Henry, a Colonial patriot who shouted, "I know not what course others may take, but as for me, give me liberty or give me death!"

The days of this kind of oratory have passed, and some of it sounds corny to us now. To use personal dedication effectively, speakers must avoid a maudlin attitude, a plea that might create an adverse reaction. But if carefully and sincerely handled, closing with an affirmation can indeed inspire other people to join you. Identification with a cause, a way of life—a belief or a commitment to a specific line of endeavor—will persuade your listeners to move in the direction you want them to go.

6. Compliment your audience. The speaking occasion often dictates the type of compliment you will use. For example, suppose you are addressing a group of leaders on the general subject of keeping the community alive and well. You are aware that the residents of this particular city have just finished a successful financial drive for their new hospital. I suggest you end your speech congratulating them on that effort. You might tie it in with this transition (a summary statement of your entire speech):

> The strength of America lies in our ability to provide a safe and healthy environment for our people...a society whose economy is strong and prosperous. Notice, I said *our ability to provide*. That does not say *our ability to beg or steal*. It does not say *our patience to wait for a handout*. I know you are people who do things for yourselves. You are *builders* and *doers*. Your successful hospital financial drive has branded you as people who care...people who can. I congratulate you for your successful completion of this task. I applaud your results and I encourage you to go on working for a growing and prosperous community.

7. Go out the same door you came in. This very persuasive technique is a magic method too often overlooked. Here's how it works: if you open with a quotation, close with it as well. If you open with a story, refer back to it as you close, even tell it again if it's short. If you open with a barrage of questions, end your speech by giving the answers.

Because the method is so simple and so readily understood, I have not bothered to present an example. I do repeat that this is a potent technique that can bring about the strong positive reaction you want from your listeners.

8. Summarize your message. Usually this implies reiteration of the main points of your speech, but don't merely rehash what you have already said. Give it a dynamic ring, an impelling urgency.

The best technique for reemphasis is to restate each of your points stressing the key words that call for action or for belief. Add encouragement to act; mention why the listeners should believe.

Another equally effective closing with the reemphasis method is to finish up with a summary paragraph that is a précis or abstract of the entire speech. Be sure to keep it persuasive. Let it reinforce your total message. Promise your audience a reward—a gain for responding affirmatively to your persuasion. Here is an example of how one speaker did it:

> Tonight we have walked down an impressive road to learn why a man succeeded in accomplishing his life mission. His profile—as a winner—can well become the matrix from which we should fashion our lives.
>
> What were the elements—the characteristics? Let's list them again—list them and burn them into our minds. The first was belief in his own self-worth and in the vitality of his mission. The second, his constant affirmation that he could reach his goal—that he would succeed. And third, a crisp, well-defined plan for reaching that goal. Finally, his personal faith and confidence in the people he worked with. Each of these is an infallible tool of success. United in his hands they became a mighty force that built a college—a living monument to a great man. Master these elements. Put them to work for yourself. They will lead you inevitably down the street of success.

By reemphasizing the points of his message, the speaker was able to review briefly the things he wanted his audience to remember. He also was able to stress the things he wanted his audience to do.

9. Visualize results. Some people call this the "threat/promise method." Be careful not to be a doom and gloom speaker. On the other hand, you can safely predict undesirable results, mission failures, or some other unwanted outcome. On the positive side, you can joyfully predict beneficial results if your advice is heeded and your course is followed.

It is possible for a speaker to use both the negative and the positive visualization techniques for maximum effectiveness. For psychological reasons, if you use both methods, be sure to end with the positive effects. Never leave the lectern with an ominous threat hanging like a black cloud in your listeners' minds.

DON'T FEEL YOUR WAY TO THE RUNWAY

We have learned nine magic ways to end a speech. A well-planned and well-directed closing is always superior to the chance landing. As a professional speaker, I once participated in a "speakers' showcase" in front of several hundred meeting planners. Each speaker on the three-day program was limited to twenty minutes. At the fifteen-minute mark, I realized I had not timed myself properly, but I wasn't concerned.

They'll let me go to twenty-five, I thought. Suddenly the timer moved toward the lectern intent on disproving my assumption. In the final frantic moments, I searched for the runway—a sentence, a quotation—anything on which I could land. In retrospect I must have appeared inept, inexperienced, and ineffectual, for my speech ended in the middle of a clumsy sentence. After thirty years of speaking professionally, I performed like a beginning student in a basic speech class.

I admit the situation was unusual, even unnatural, but it illustrates how a speech can go awry without a well-planned, well-executed ending. The personal embarrassment can be endured and forgotten, but the failure to accomplish your effect, to add the magic power of persuasion, is inexcusable—a lost opportunity that can never be regained.

LET'S PRACTICE

Skill Builders

1. Select a persuasive point in which you believe strongly. Suggestions (or make up one of your own):

Women in industry are not treated fairly.
Money alone never motivates a worker.
A government cannot spend its way to prosperity.
Open competition stimulates industrial success.

State your point and then conclude it by using each of the nine methods described previously. Transitions are important. You may find it easier to talk about your point for a moment and bring it to life for yourself. Then move gracefully into whatever concluding technique you are using—an illustration, an appeal, reemphasis, or whatever you have chosen.

2. Using the same point, try to end your speech with as many different techniques as you can.

3. Select your favorite speech from your files. Stand up (in front of the mirror, if you wish) and give the part of your speech that leads to the conclusion. Develop and practice as many different endings as you can, using one or more of the nine methods described in this chapter. Put all of your persuasive power into the closing. Remember that the ending is the very last tap that drives home your message.

Singers, actors, and speakers share a common desire: to leave the audience with a favorable impression. Standing ovations are outward expressions of audience appreciation. Speakers should plan the final moments of the speech to draw a positive and enthusiastic response from their listeners. We aren't necessarily looking for a standing ovation, but we do want the audience to believe us and to accept our ideas. A powerful, persuasive ending brings those results—and often may elicit the ovation as well.

SUCCESS SECRET: A speaker who runs down at the end is like a piano player who stops three measures away from the last note.

PRESS THE MAGIC-MEMORY STAMP

Don't leave the ending of your speech to chance. It should be the climax of your persuasive effectiveness. It is the clincher to your speech.

Following are some common faults in unplanned endings:

1. *Trailaway endings.* They have no planned closing spot.
2. *New-idea endings.* The speaker keeps floating away from the ending as fresh material flows into his mind.
3. *Chopped-off endings.* Without warning, without clues, the speaker stops, leaving his listeners totally bewildered.
4. *Endless-promise endings.* The speaker tells us many times that he's going to stop, but he can't seem to find the landing strip. Listeners are left edgy and sometimes angry.

End your speech with a power punch. Use one or more of these effective methods:

1. *Ask for action.* Call for the order.
2. *Wrap it up with humor.* A bit of irony or a funny story might provide the punch you need.
3. *Finish with a dramatic incident.* The theme of your message embodied in a gripping tale can be the ultimate in persuasion.
4. *Close with an illustration, a quotation, or a poem.* Over the years hundreds of effective speakers have discovered how to close with a persuasive example, a compelling quotation, or a powerful bit of verse.
5. *Commit yourself to the mission you advocate.* Establish yourself with your audience, then become a persuasive leader by committing yourself to action. It's a magic method.
6. *Close with a compliment to your audience.* Be real, be genuine, and you'll automatically be effective.

7. *Go out the same door you came in.* Audiences respond positively to this technique. Returning to the familiar ring of your opening remarks can be an emphatic way to end your speech.

8. *Summarize your message.* Repetition is an age-old method of gaining belief. Tell your audience what you've said. Summarize it with a dynamic, persuasive ring.

9. *End the speech by visualizing results.* Show what good things will occur if your ideas are followed. Show the unfavorable things that might accrue if your ideas are shunned.

Inject all of your persuasive power into the closing. Remember that this is the last punch you get to drive your message home.

A LOOK AHEAD

Language is fundamental to all persuasion. *How you say it* makes all the difference in the world and may be of equal importance to *what you say.* The art of interesting expression and verbal imagery can be readily learned. Simply learn to choose energetic words and use them in lively sentences. Draw comparisons. Paint figures of speech. Call on the host of other verbal techniques that are the secrets of personal persuasion. At the same time, strive for clear expression by chopping the clutter from your speech. *Say what you mean and say it well.*

In the next chapter these secrets will be revealed.

chapter 4

How to Persuade with Verbal Magic

Winston Churchill was a master of the English language. He didn't label his communications tools or specifically identify his techniques, but you can be sure that Old Winnie's techniques can be of use to us if we study his words, spoken at a time of serious national crisis:

> Never in the field of human conflict was so much owed by so many to so few.
>
> *(The Battle of Britain—Speech in the House of Commons, 20 August, 1940)*

> We shall defend our island, whatever the cost may be, we shall fight on the beaches, we shall fight on the landing grounds, we shall fight in the fields and in the streets, we shall fight in the hills; we shall never surrender.
>
> *(Speech in the House of Commons, 4 June, 1940)*

> Let us...so bear ourselves that, if the British ...Commonwealth last for a thousand years, men will still say: "This was their finest hour."
>
> *(Speech in the House of Commons, 18 June, 1940)*

Reach for these personal persuasion goals in this chapter:

1. Choose and use precise vocabulary. Say exactly what you mean with the specific words that say it best.

2. Explore the subject of *picture words*. Acquire the magic art of concrete expression without sounding fake or unreal.

ESCAPE THE TRAP OF WEARY WORDS

It is not the purpose of this book to indict modern communicators, but there are many who abuse our language. Every speaker and conversationalist should recognize the degenerate expressions that surround us—the blight that has infected our beautiful language. Through mass communications, a misused and weary vocabulary quickly reaches the multitudes who immediately imitate and repeat what they have heard. Substandard words quietly gain respectability by taking squatters' rights in an authoritative dictionary. Teachers, legislators, pastors, and business executives all spread the disease of flimsy, constricted vocabulary and meaningless jargon.

Because most of us are exposed to this constant barrage of coined and flabby expressions, it's easy to succumb to the gobbledygook syndrome. Be effective in your personal persuasion by insulating yourself against nonsense vocabulary and patterned conversation.

> **SUCCESS SECRET: Learn to recognize weak expressions and find a better way to say it.**

I do make this admission: Some of our most tired clichés were once clever, inventive figures of speech. As the masses assimilated them, however, a million mouths began to spew them out. Quickly the words and phrases became burned-out language bums.

The following are some examples.

1. A creative mind once said, "You have reinvented the wheel." This clever figure of speech says so much, but what has happened to it? People have worked it to death. I emit

a low groan when I hear people say, at least once a week, "Let's not reinvent the wheel."

Essentially the same thing happened to the expression, "I need to know where you are coming from." This comment has also gone stale.

2. And here is another: The word *impact* was once used only as a noun. (Americans like to make verbs out of nouns, perhaps a tribute to the flexibility of our great language.) One day, someone transformed *impact* into an effective verb. Through overuse it has become an incompetent substitute for other, far better verbs. Newscasters, magazine writers, seminar leaders, and scores of conversationalists tell us about "decisions that impact on our economy," or on whatever else they can *impact* on.

More weary and faddish expressions to avoid:

You are comparing apples to oranges.	Fantastic!
	Super!
To talk honestly...	Let's try it and see if it flies.
Be that as it may...	If you'll permit me...
Hopefully...	It gives me great pleasure...
Firstly, secondly	It's really terrific!

> **SUCCESS SECRET: Create your own original figures of speech and leave the clichés to someone else.**

REAP PERSUASIVE POWER WITH WALLOPING WORDS

For clear communication, a sentence needs only a subject and a verb. If the subject is understood or implied, the verb alone is enough.

"Go!" says it all.

You can't go around speaking in one-word sentences, but you can improve your skill by going back to the fundamental sentence, which has a subject, a verb, probably a modifier or two, and an object.

"The man walked home."

Here you find all of the basic ingredients. Identify sentence components and word relationships. Whenever possible, speak in the active voice. When the subject acts on the predicate, you sound vibrant. Your expression is strong, confident, and persuasive.

To gain strength, pick the most specific noun available. In the sentence example above, *man* is a general term. Substitute a proper noun, perhaps some well-known person whom your listeners can visualize. This adds strength to your statement. If you can't use a proper noun, at least add a colorful adjective. Let the man be *gray-haired,* or verbally dress him in *blue jeans.* Make him *tall,* or *bent,* or *shriveled.* These words create mental pictures.

Now, let's dress up the verb: Let the gray-haired man *shuffle, stagger, limp,* or *sway.* You have added another dimension.

> **SUCCESS SECRET: A word is dull if it fails to do one of the following: imply action, paint a mental picture, or evoke a physical or psychological stirring.**

Be sure that you don't use adjectives and adverbs merely to prop up your main words like two-by-fours holding up the walls of a house. Make the walls strong, then add the cosmetic supports that contribute image and energy to your conversation or your speech.

> **SUCCESS SECRET: Such words as very, quite, and somewhat are weak supports that hold up helpless expressions. Find strong verbs or adjectives so you won't need useless props.**

Even dry statistics take on luster and clarity if handled creatively. I once heard a speaker say, "If the national debt were changed into silver dollars and stacked one on top of the other, the stacks would reach seven-and-a-half times to the moon." Convert sterile numbers into a form your listeners can visualize. This is called *concrete expression*. Create a structure. Lay pieces end to end or translate the numbers into a pie and cut it into component parts. Mileage in unfamiliar regions can be equated with the distance from a geographical point your listeners are acquainted with.

Even a graph or a chart is better than an oral recitation of meaningless numbers.

> **SUCCESS SECRET: To communicate abstract figures, give them shapes. Create a mental picture your listeners can refer to.**

ENRICH YOUR VOCABULARY BANK

Persuasive, clear communication requires a broad vocabulary. Do you find yourself progressively losing your storehouse of words? Most people do after leaving school, but you can easily reverse the trend.

Carry a small dictionary with you—to lunch, on the plane—wherever you might find a quiet moment to fill the vocabulary well. Don't waste time learning long, obscure words. Pick the shorter image-builders. Run your eyes down the columns of beautiful words, unmined jewels that plead with you to use them. You already understand most of them. Over the years, you have merely filed them away in some obscure compartment of the brain, so they no longer tumble out when you need them in conversation or on the platform. Too often you have replaced them with more accessible, hack substitutes: *swell, terrific, fantastic, great, really,* and *you know.*

Bring out those former good-friend words. Let them work for you, words that tickle and prickle, scratch and scrape, move and smooth, chuckle and churn. They stand by waiting for you to blend them into lively patterns.

Here are some sample helpers (words that seem to speak):

ablaze	dupe	gilt
adorn	dusky	glum
agile	dwarf	glut
amble	eager	gory
ashen	ebb	grasp
awkward	echo	grim
azure	elastic	gully
bald	empty	gusty
barren	enjoy	hack
barter	etch	hanker
bicker	excite	hardy
blur	fable	harsh
bold	failing	hazy
brawl	fallow	hermit
cackle	fancy	hump
caress	fang	hush
chubby	farce	idle
clamor	fetch	idol
clang	fib	jam
claws	fidget	jolly
clip	fiery	jolt
clutch	filth	jostle
coast	fizz	joy
cozy	foggy	juggle
creamy	folly	junk
crusty	foolish	keen
cunning	frantic	lackey
dabble	frill	lag
dainty	fritter	lanky
dangle	fudge	leaden
debris	gad	leaky
dewy	gait	lean
dim	gale	loaf
dismal	gall	lofty
dull	garb	lout
dunce	ghastly	lumpy

lurch	poke	tangled
lurk	prattle	tarnished
magic	prod	tender
meek	quest	throb
mire	quirk	trashy
mirth	retreat	turf
mist	rift	ugly
moan	rigging	uncoil
mulish	roam	vacant
munch	rowdy	vandal
myth	rugged	vassal
nag	rustle	venom
nasty	rut	vexed
nibble	sag	waft
nip	sallow	waif
nudge	savage	wail
numb	scoff	warp
ogre	scorn	weep
orgy	scrawl	whack
oust	scum	winnow
pagan	shadowy	wither
pallor	shifty	wretched
panic	shun	writhe
parched	slam	yearn
peep	slime	yelp
petal	smirk	yokel
pirate	snarl	zenith
plodder	soggy	zip
plunge	sulky	

Let this be the beginning of your word diary. Listen for words that seem to speak. How many different ways can you use them? For example, the word *fallow* most often refers to fields, but minds can lie fallow. So can a friendship. How else can you use the word to give it an unusual twist? My personal word diary doesn't necessarily contain long, rare, or difficult words. The four- and five-letter ones are best. My list includes expressive boosters that I might forget to use if I didn't have them written down. I review the list frequently just to keep the words fresh and active. The more often I look at them, the more readily they volunteer for duty when I'm in conversation in the conference room or at the lectern facing an audience.

Remember: Vocabulary coupled with a lively imagination is the key to personal persuasion. Verbal brushes paint indelible pictures in the human mind. Replace your shapeless abstractions with concrete words that are vibrant and expressive. Creative use of the language is the badge of personal professionalism.

One of the finest books on the subject of clear, concrete expression was written by William Strunk, Jr. and E. B. White. *Elements of Style* is a small book that you will devour quickly. Once you have read it, you will return again and again for repeated refreshment. Pick up a copy. I guarantee you will cherish it.

> **SUCCESS SECRET: Use vigorous sentences, galloping ones that say what you mean instead of sluggish phrases that say nothing and go nowhere.**

LEARN THE LANGUAGE OF YOUR LISTENERS

Every profession and every craft has its nomenclature, its own distinctive terms and language. Using the vocabulary of the trade can provide instant audience interest, respect, and confidence. The method isn't difficult. Develop a short glossary of terms that your listeners might use in their daily work. Speak their language. You will be amazed at how many comparisons, similes, and metaphors you can invent. Even your illustrations, your quotations, and your humor can be readily adapted with a bit of thought and practice. For example:

"Architects insert keystones that hold their organization together."

"Executives need *down time* in their mental computers to restore production efficiency."

In a speech to an engineering society, instead of using an attorney in your illustration, substitute an engineer. Replace the lawyer's brief with a blueprint. Instead of words like logic or evidence, talk about "...laying one brick on top of another" to reach a conclusion or to establish a principle.

For a few days, practice translating your ideas into analogies that apply to the work and professional terms of the listeners, no matter what their walk of life: teachers, farmers, plumbers, dentists, or business executives.

CHOP THE CLUTTER—ORGANIZE YOUR IDEAS

Have you ever tried to explain a process or an idea you didn't understand? Somehow, instead of ringing clear, the explanation emerges as a tangled string of meaningless words and unrelated sentences. Your comments lack structure and precision.

From my own experience, here is a good example. I was to speak at a meeting in Washington, D.C. on a promotion project, a subject on which I was considered an authority. A delay in my flight from Minneapolis resulted in my late arrival at the meeting. I no sooner joined the group at the conference table than a member hurled a difficult question at me. My mind was still in neutral, or perhaps locked in "park."

As an "authority," my ego demanded that I respond. My answer was a classic example of *response without understanding*. For two minutes I spoke rapidly and said nothing. In retrospect I should merely have said, "Please

let me listen for a while until I have some background on
your discussion."

> **SUCCESS SECRET: Ideas are like good wine. They
> must be given time to ferment before they are poured.**

An attempt to impress your listeners can often lead to
poor communication. Obscure language—lack of precision, excessive words—clutters the channels and interferes
with personal persuasion.

At a meeting in New Orleans, a prestigious speaker
presented a thorough analysis of international politics to a
well-educated audience. At the end of his speech he invited
members of the audience to ask questions. In back of the
room, a gentleman rose and asked, "Sir, what is our
national goal? Is it to force the communist nation to return
to its preinvasion confines, or to dissuade her from repeating the bellicose actions at some future time in history and
at some other vulnerable location?"

Obviously the question was fraught with complex
words. Without sarcasm or ridicule, the speaker simplified
it quickly by saying, "The question was, 'Do we want
Russia to leave Afghanistan or to keep her troops at home
from now on?'"

> **SUCCESS SECRET: Say it. Don't say around it.**

BUILD FROM A CLEAR IDEA

Whether you rise to speak in church, participate in
discussion at a staff meeting, or engage in simple dialogue
with your supervisor, there is an effective way to organize
your material for greatest impact. Practice using the
method and observe how much the quality of your personal persuasion improves.

How to do it

In a concise, clear sentence, state the point you want to make. Be sure it is narrow and specific—not general or abstract. Run the point through your mind. Do you understand it? Until you do, you aren't ready to speak. Here are some examples of points to make:

People no longer care about productive performance.

Speech training helps people organize their thoughts.

Bill Jacobs is a good welder.

The church should avoid political involvement.

Government regulations reduce business profits.

A sixteen-year-old should not be allowed to take the car to an out-of-town football game.

These clear statements are ready to be supported. They are points you might need to prove on the platform, in the board room, at church, or even in family discussions. Imperfect attempts at persuasion begin with improperly conceived foundation points. *Fix the point in your mind; then proceed to nail it down.* Be sure you believe what you have to say. *Personal belief and personal persuasion have a strong affinity* for each other.

Example: Marjory's Situation

Your supervisor asks, "Marjory, why should we continue to operate a darkroom in your department?" (Take your time, Marjory. Don't answer immediately. If you need time to prepare your answer, acknowledge that this is an important question, one that requires careful evaluation and perhaps some research. Remember, by asking for time, you are demonstrating caution and thoroughness, not fear. Your unwillingness to provide a superficial answer in itself should enhance your personal effectiveness. If the question is one you can answer at once, go ahead as soon as you have let your material ferment. Phrase your answer in a crisp persuasive statement, then add the support.)

Marjory's Response

"The darkroom has saved our company thousands of dollars." (Here is a strong point, a promise of putting dollars in the company's operating statement. Now Marjory is ready to bolster the point with an example.) "The audio-visual people saved one day's wages by being able to process film at once rather than waiting twenty-four hours to have it done by a commercial developer." (She might provide comparisons between the total cost of a company operated darkroom and the expense of paying for an outside service. Select accurate, believable evidence that shows why the darkroom is financially advantageous. A quotation from the controller would certainly enhance Marjory's contention. She might think of many other ways to gain acceptance for her belief, but she should pick only what is needed to make the point and save the rest for later ammunition if needed.)

SUCCESS SECRET: Never oversell your point.

Here is a good check method for using support. After stating your point, insert (either orally or mentally) the word *because* or the words *for example*. If your proof material flows naturally from either of these, you are doing it properly. Meet this test and you automatically have a good chance for acceptance.

LET'S PRACTICE

Skill Builders

To stretch your word power, spend three minutes every day scanning the word columns in your dictionary. Many words that are old friends will reenter your mind. Start using them again as often as possible.

Keep a list of words you want to recall. Select those that touch the senses—*warm, rough, smooth, quiet, thump, clang, sweet, noisy*—picture words you can feel and taste and see and smell. To assimilate them thoroughly, practice *mind-talking*—making mental sentences to see how many ways you can verbally create a sight or a sensation.

Describe a section of an unusual wall, a piece of sandpaper, a lake, or a sunset over a field of grain. Scan the faces in a crowd. What details do you see? What do they remind you of? Look at a street during a downpour. Does the water ripple, sparkle, babble, and splash? Shut your eyes and conjure up a lake. Is it like blue crystal reflecting dancing sunlight? Or more slate-colored like a stormy sky?

Make a one-point statement that needs proof. Keep rewording until it is clear and brief. Phrase it so that people will be inclined to accept it automatically. Give it a beneficial ring. Let the noun and verb literally pop out and clutch people. Then add an example that makes it even more believable. Keep thinking of new ways to prove it.

At the end of a week, state your point aloud and follow it with the examples, quotations, and statistics you feel are most effective. Stand in front of a mirror and pretend you are on the platform speaking to an audience. Now sit down and make believe you are presenting the same point to a supervisor or fellow worker sitting across the table from you. Repeat this experience, ad-lib, using the same material for one week. Next, retain the same point, but substitute new material. Practice it aloud every day standing in front of your make-believe audience or sitting beside your make-believe supervisor. It also helps to say it silently one or two times each day, perhaps as you walk or as you are driving to work.

PRESS THE MAGIC-MEMORY STAMP

Avoid using weary words. Remove them from your vocabulary. Give life and sparkle to your speech by using specific nouns and action-packed verbs. Add color words, but don't use them as crutches for tired nouns or verbs.

Learn to build mental images with the words you choose—words that transmit feeling messages. Help your listeners visualize shapes and colors, experience pain or joy, feel surfaces, hear music, smell odors, and taste the substances your words suggest.

A LOOK AHEAD

We are ready to work with your voice. Our objectives are

1. To improve vocal quality.
2. To make words crisp and understandable.
3. To acquire the "natural sound" needed for sincere delivery of your material.

By learning to regulate your rate, pitch, and volume, you will project accurate meaning and genuine feeling into your sentences.

Personal persuasion improves as you enrich your vocal mechanism. The secrets for attaining these objectives are revealed in Chapter 5.

chapter 5

Develop a Persuasive Voice

"Is that my voice?" most of us exclaim when we hear ourselves for the first time on a tape recorder. People seldom sound as they think they should, but after the initial shock they usually become accustomed to "sounding that way."

SUCCESS SECRET: The tape recorder is a superior tool for vocal improvement.

Remember that word, *improvement*. Don't be discouraged if you don't sound like your favorite anchorperson. You probably never will. Instead let your goal be to improve, and to sound your own very best.

In this chapter you will learn

1. To sound natural and sincere.
2. To relax the throat for comfort and for a pleasant tone—a desirable quality.
3. To use the Success Secret Tools—pitch, rate, and volume (PRV).
4. To articulate in a natural way.
5. To create a flexible, expressive voice.

Let's get started on this fun-filled experience in personal persuasion.

LISTEN TO HOW YOU SOUND

The tape never lies. Record your practice sessions to accelerate improvement. At first you may not like what you hear. Although Nature endowed most of us with remarkably good voices, the first encounter with a tape recorder is a nasty shock. The reason is simple enough: We hear ourselves subjectively, from the inside. The recording reaches us aurally; that is, through the outer ear. The tone or quality of these two voices is strikingly different.

Quality is the characteristic sound of your voice. It is the attribute that makes YOU sound like YOU. There are many different kinds of vocal quality—some of them extremely unpleasant like the squeaker, the gravel voice, the breathy whisper. Of course there is also the tone we all want: the full, rich, and resonant voice.

By listening to these different kinds of voices, the good and the bad, and by practicing, you will begin to acquire an ear for good tones and identify acceptable standards. Strive to sound the best you can. Keep practicing. Improvement may be gradual, but it will be progressive.

As you proceed, be careful you don't become a *phony-toney*. It is easy to practice your way into unnatural sounds. Naturalness never calls attention to itself but affectation does—whether it is the use of long *aaah* improperly replacing the regular *ay*, or a fake intonation that gushes out leaving you and your listeners gasping for air.

I acknowledge that Nature prescribed a certain vocal quality for you by designing your throat, your mouth, and your nose. These physical areas affect the tone of your voice the same as the size and shape of resonating surfaces affect the quality of a stereo system. But don't resign yourself to having less than you can possess. Practice the exercises in the Skill Builders section of this chapter to strengthen your voice and bring out its most positive characteristics. After that, quit fussing about it.

The music of your voice comes largely from the vowel sounds and the nasals. (The nasal sounds come through your nose). To enrich your tones, let the vowels swell out; give them free rein.

Don't constrict the nasals. Let them resonate through your mouth and sinus areas. You've heard people say, "He talks through his nose." Most often this isn't the case at all. When the sounds are not properly amplified in the nasal passages, the person is *denasal*.

To improve your vocal quality

1. Learn to recognize different kinds of voices and avoid sounds that are unpleasant: raspy, breathy, denasal, gravelly.
2. Relax your throat whenever you talk.
3. Don't mutter. Open your mouth and let the sounds flow out.
4. Keep your pitch as low as you can without straining your voice.

SUCCESS SECRET: Low pitches usually create better tones than high pitches.

GET ACQUAINTED WITH PRV

Your voice has controls very similar to those on a car. By using the gas pedal, the steering wheel, and the brake, you can make your automobile speed up, turn, slow down, or stop. In much the same way, PRV (pitch, rate, and volume) alters the voice to reflect feeling and direct meaning.

One step at a time, let's see how PRV works. Human feelings are not necessarily experienced in extremes; that is, you aren't either sad or happy, glum or excited, loving or hate-filled. Ordinarily you are at a point on the scale or spectrum somewhere between these opposites. In other words you usually experience varying degrees of feelings instead of the extremes. But to help you grasp the meaning of PRV and capture the ability to use them, we must assume there is a clearcut dividing line between the *subdued emotions* (sadness, love, depression, and so forth) and the *animated feelings* (happiness, joy, hatred, and so forth.) Sadness, then, would be the opposite of joy, love the opposite of hatred, and depression the opposite of excitement.

Got it? The SUBDUED EMOTIONS and the ANIMATED FEELINGS. Now you are ready to observe some very interesting things about your voice. Invariably it tips off the kind of feeling you are experiencing at any given moment. In personal persuasion this is important for two reasons:

1. Your voice reflects your moods and controls your PRV.

2. PRV transfers that same mood to your listeners.

I admit that some people can fake a mood and deceive their listeners, but faking a mood is not an honest communication procedure.

> **SUCCESS SECRET: Sincerity is a speaker's best friend. It bolsters reputation and becomes a trademark of excellence in personal persuasion on the platform, in the boardroom, or around the family table.**

Now let's get on with a specific discussion of PRV. We'll begin with the following definitions:

Pitch is the highness or lowness of your voice. It also makes up the melody of your speech.

Rate is the speed at which you transmit words.

Volume is the loudness level of your voice.

To help you understand PRV I shall isolate each of the factors and describe it separately so you can learn how it works and how it influences your communication;

however, remember that *the PRV factors are never isolated in the speaking process.* Vary one and you automatically change the others. All of them, in concert, reflect your feelings. For example, if you are sad, you speak in a low tone with a narrow range, at a slow rate, and with the volume turned down. Conversely, if you are excited, the pitch rises, your range spreads, you speak rapidly and very loudly—sometimes with the volume up full blast.

As you will see later, *meaning* is also influenced by how you handle PRV.

HOW TO REGULATE YOUR PITCH

To obtain a feel for pitch movement, extend your arm in front of your midsection with the palm of your hand turned downwards. Say a word, any word. Now say it again, but raise your hand five or six inches and *lift the pitch of your voice with it.* Now, starting with a low note, climb the scale while moving the hand and voice upward in unison. Up the ladder you go, one note at a time. (Move the hand about three inches for each note.) Now come down the ladder. Feel it? Hear it? This is a splendid exercise for detecting pitch changes.

Most of us have a range of about seven tones. These notes are the equivalent of the *white keys* on a piano. Effective speakers and conversationalists also use the five tones indicated by the *black keys*. See if you can hear these notes as you listen to professional actors and speakers. A good ear is essential for learning. Listen to others. You will hear the good as well as the fake. Notice especially how people reflect feelings and moods by key changes in their voices. And the best part is that neither the speaker nor the listeners are aware that the pitch change occurred at all.

Some dos and don'ts

1. Don't be a "Billy one-note." His last name is Monotone. He's boring.

2. Don't gush or let your pitch gallop up and down the scale in a hyperdramatic charge.

3. Avoid pitch patterns—the habit of starting and ending every sentence on the same note or intoning every sentence with the same repetitious melody.

4. Avoid the "politician's intonation." It follows a three or four note pitch pattern accompanied by an overstressing of nouns and verbs. Listen for it on the radio or on television, then reject it at once as inferior communication.

HOW TO CONTROL YOUR RATE

Most people speak at a rate somewhere between one hundred and one hundred twenty words a minute. The speech rate can be adjusted in either of two ways or by a combination of these methods.

1. By prolonging the continuant sounds: the vowels, the nasals, and the consonants like *f, v, s,* and *z.* Notice you cannot sustain a *t, d, p, b, g,* or *k.* These are *stopped consonants* made by an explosion of trapped air.

2. By pausing between words or groups of words (phrases, clauses, or sentences).

We are now ready to see how properly controlled rate can express feeling, reinforcing the effect of pitch. Suppose you are sympathizing with a friend who has lost her father. You won't reel off as fast as you can talk, "Gee, Deanna, I'm sorry your father died." Not at all. You'll speak slowly. "Deanna ... I'm ... sorry about ... your father." Your voice slows down naturally. You hang onto the vowels. You pause between words.

If you are excited, angry, or afraid, you perform in an opposite way. Your words tumble out. You clip the sounds. You seldom hesitate or pause. In part, that's why people run out of breath in the animated moods. They don't stop long enough to replenish their air supply. In the Skill Builders section of this chapter you'll learn to control rate effectively.

HOW TO ADJUST THE VOLUME CONTROL

One of the first rules of volume is the *rule of audibility.* If you cannot be heard, don't bother to speak. How often have you sat in meetings or in conversations and tried to decipher the mutterer. Don't be one of them. Hold your chin at a right angle to the throat. Steer your voice towards your listeners.

Years ago one of my speech teachers instructed us, "Bounce your voice off the back wall of the classroom!" It was one of the greatest vocal lessons I have ever had.

Volume, like pitch and rate, can help you to express feelings. It's obvious that subdued feelings are never screamed (not naturally, anyway) and animated feelings can hardly be contained within a mutter. You can learn from the little kids! Youngsters give good lessons in vocal control. A tiny voice reflects naturally the way a youngster feels deep inside.

PUT MEANING IN YOUR VOICE

So far you have concentrated on how the voice captures and reflects feelings. PRV can also highlight ideas, making them stand out and grasp attention.

Let's see how it works. Suppose you want to emphasize an idea. Try pausing a second before you say it. At the same time, change pitch and state the idea very slowly. Notice how your listeners prick up their ears and become attentive. Now with the same idea, change pitch and pause, but say the idea louder. Notice that it still gains attention. This is a strange thing about idea highlighting:

It isn't the *type* of change that matters; it's the *change* itself.

Practice and listen. You'll soon discover how to make you ideas stand out in the crowd.

Peculiar things your voice can do: There are subtle techniques for conveying meaning and revealing mental attitudes through pitch. You are familiar with the rising voice at the end of a question. Are you also aware that *uncertainty* is expressed in the same way? So is *disbelief.* In an opposite vein, *surety, finality,* and *stern commands* are expressed with a downward glide on the final word in a sentence or clause.

Your meaning can also be expressed by the way you stress a word within a sentence. Try this: "I am going to the downtown theater." Hit the first word, "*I.*" Now stress the second word, "*am.*" Now the third. Obviously, your meaning changes as you hit different words. What you are really doing is varying the volume on the word you are stressing. (Automatically a pitch movement occurs as well.)

As you work with the Skill Builders near the end of the chapter, you will develop a good ear for sound and voice. Soon your ear will catch the nuances of feeling and meaning that the voice is able to communicate expertly.

FORM YOUR WORDS THE NATURAL WAY

Two speakers, each using the same public address system, may obtain noticeably different results. The reason for the variance is a skill called *articulation.* PA systems can fail; they can *create* distortion, but they can never *correct* it. If sounds are garbled when they leave the speaker's mouth, they'll still be garbled when they reach the listener's ears.

Each sound in our language is made in a specific way by the organs of articulation—primarily the teeth, the tongue, the palate, and the lips. There is also a tiny flap at the top of the throat, called the uvula, that creates some sounds.

Although it's not necessary to know how sounds are formed, I have discovered that diction improves more rapidly when people understand the phonetic construction of consonants. (I have specified consonants because they convey the meaning in our language. Vowels transmit its beauty.)

WHAT YOU NEED TO KNOW ABOUT CONSONANTS

Consonant sounds are born in either of two ways: (1) by forcing air over a surface in the mouth, or (2) by trapping air momentarily and then exploding it. The first type of consonant is called a *continuant* and the second type is called a *stopped consonant* or *plosive*.

Most consonants are twins, or companions; that is, they are identical except for the presence or absence of vocal cord vibration. For example, *z* and *s* are a pair formed by grooving the tongue, arching it slightly, and then blowing air against the cutting edge of the bottom teeth. The vocal cords vibrate on *z* but not on *s*. To verify this dissimilarity, gently grasp the top of your throat between your thumb and forefinger. Alternately sound *z* and *s*. You'll physically feel the difference. *V* and *f* are also companions made by placing the lower lip against the cutting edge of the upper teeth and letting air escape from the corners of the mouth. *V* vibrates; *f* does not.

> **SUCCESS SECRET:** The sounds *z*, *s*, *v* and *f* are made by a friction or hissing of air. Usually they are unpleasant sounds that should not be prolonged.

There are six *stopped* consonants: *b, p, d, t, g,* and *k.* The *b* and *p* sounds are formed by trapping air behind compressed lips and then exploding it. *B* vibrates, but *p* does not.

The plosives *d* and *t* are made by blocking air with the tongue against the palate above the upper teeth, then letting it "explode." In this pair, only the *d* vibrates.

Can you now determine how the *g* and *k* are trapped? Which of the pair is accompanied by vibration of the vocal cords? By experimenting with your tongue as you form various sounds you'll readily be able to discover how they are made.

Let's explore a few more consonants. An *r* is a continuant made by tapping the tongue against the upper palate—just like a *d*, except the air is not blocked. Some people can trill an *r* by rapidly tapping the tongue against the gum ridge. An *l* is made much like the *r* except air slides off the sides of the tongue.

Earlier, you used the nasal sounds *m*, *n*, and *ng* as quality builders. These three sounds actually pass through your nose. Let them resonate freely for pleasing sounds.

Now locate these sounds in your mouth: *y, h, j, q, w,* and *x*. Notice that some sounds are combinations of two or more letters. For example, *q* is really *kyu* blended rapidly. *X* is *eks. Wh*, as in *what*, is pronounced in a reverse position as *hwat*.

Clear enunciation and a good blend of sounds are necessary for personal persuasion. Do not neglect the consonants if you want to be understood. A lazy tongue is common in American speech. A typical conversation might go like this:

"Hi! Jeat?"

"Yep."

"Wa' ja' have?"

"'Neg 'n' apple."

Properly spoken:

"Hi! Did you eat?"

"Yes."

"What did you have?"

"An egg and an apple."

SUCCESS SECRET: Good diction is a prize to be sought. Overprecision is a plague to be shunned.

No matter what the cause of fuzzy speech, you won't learn to crisp your words until you can hear the error of your sounds. In the magic Skill Builder you will find exercises to improve even the most stubborn cases of unclear speech.

Bounce Your Voice off the Back Wall

You may want to try my speech teacher's technique of trying to bounce your voice off the back wall. It won't hurt you and it might be beneficial. At any rate, avoid cramping your voice inside a "bent throat." Just as an electronics expert points his loudspeakers toward the crowd, so the public speaker points his lips toward the listeners. Not only does this send the sound the way it ought to go, but it also prevents kinking in your neck. Point your voice at your listeners. Don't be like the hunter who repeatedly shot his gun into the air, confident that a duck would eventually fly into the shot. Point your voice where your listeners are and reap a rich harvest of audience responses.

LET'S PRACTICE

Skill Builders

Spend a few minutes each day doing the exercises you need most. I do voice exercises without effort while driving alone in the car or while alone in my office.

To improve voice quality

1. Slide up and down the scale on each vowel sound—*oo* as in *pool*, *aa* as in *fall*, *ee* as in *feel*, *u* as in *up*—while keeping the voice relaxed and comfortable

2. Hum each of the nasals, *m*, *n*, and *ng*, in sequence, softly at first, then letting the sound swell. Hold the sound at full volume for a moment, then let it gradually fade.

To give strength to your voice

1. Relax the throat. Without strain, say *ha ha*. Start softly, then gradually shout louder and louder. Stop when you feel strain or soreness in the throat.

2. Start softly with a prolonged *ee* sound. Swell it. Diminish it. Try stepping to different pitch levels. Now glide from one pitch to another as you build the volume.

Remember to avoid strain during both these exercises.

To improve articulation

1. Read slowly from any prose passage. Carefully *overpronounce* each letter to be sounded. Be overly precise as you read.

2. Loosen the tongue with a good tongue twister. Each time you repeat it, accelerate the recitation *but never slur the words*. Try these twisters and also collect some of your own:

Betty bought some bitter butter. She put it in the better batter, and it made the better batter bitter; so, Betty bought some better butter, put it in the bitter batter and it made the bitter batter better.

and

The sea, she ceaseth us and yet sufficeth us.

To put meaning and feeling in your speech

1. Make believe that someone has just told you an incredible fact. Express your surprise or disbelief. Try the

sentence, "Mary Jones embezzled money." Using the same sentence, say it as if your mind has just accepted the truth of the statement.

2. Express disbelief by gliding on the word *oh*. Using the same word, express surprise. Now, comprehension. Next, disappointment.

3. Using the sentence, "I...take a job in Brazil," express surprise, indignation, and determination. Notice, with a bit of practice, that precise meanings come through by the way you handle PRV.

PRESS THE MAGIC-MEMORY STAMP

The tape recorder provides an accurate image of your voice. *What you hear is what you have.* Become used to it. To improve your voice, keep listening and practicing, then quit fussing about it.

Strive always to be natural. Avoid phony patterns and artificial tones.

PRV will help you transmit feeling through your words. For subdued feelings restrict the range, slow the rate, and reduce the loudness. Quality responds with a full, rich tone. Animated moods require an opposite treatment with PRV. Quality responds usually with a more raucous, sometimes raspy sound.

Use pitch, rate, and volume to transfer meaning through your words. A rising pitch implies question, uncertainty, disbelief. Descending glides show finality, positiveness, declaration. Develop a pleasing melody.

Pausing before you express an idea (rate control) spotlights it for your listeners. Changing the volume, either louder or softer, also highlights an idea. A change of PRV always emphasizes your statement regardless of which way the change is made. Remember, be natural at all times.

Crisp articulation is accomplished by proper and careful formation of the consonants. Slovenly articulation and overpreciseness are both to be avoided.

A LOOK AHEAD

Body communication has long been an art. In recent years the masses have become increasingly aware of its importance and have made diligent efforts to learn body language techniques.

In the next chapter you will discover how your body actually "talks," either as a substitute for words or to reinforce the things you are saying. You will learn the secrets of body communication.

chapter 6

Persuade with Body
Communication

Speak not with words alone. Let the language of your body help you to persuade.

Observe the deaf. They possess a language all their own—impressive, animated, communicative. Using the body to supplement your voice adds a second dimension to your speech. Like the deaf, your body can truly talk if you'll only let it!

You begin the persuasive process the moment you enter the room or the auditorium, especially if you are a stranger. At the head table or on the platform, meet the audience with a magic smile. Right now, this moment, people are looking at you, appraising you, forming opinions about the kind of person you are. And the conclusion they reach makes all the difference in the world.

I learned this fact the hard way. One night after I had finished a speech, a lady from the audience said to me, "Say, you really come to life when the spotlight hits you." I probed for an explanation, and she shared it generously: "You looked so glum sitting at the head table." (She wasn't sufficiently candid to say "bored," but bored is how I had looked.) The lady did me a favor. From then on, I remembered to smile and to avoid faraway expressions even while mentally rehearsing my speech.

SUCCESS SECRET: Replace the rigid jaw with a relaxed smile. Don't chomp impatiently as you await your turn to speak.

When I begin my speech or conversation, I need to respect my listeners if they are to respect me. The circular response works on this principle. Never defeat yourself before you begin. Never telegraph the impression that your speech is the only worthwhile thing on the program or your opinion the only one that counts in a meeting. Look interested, and you will be interesting. Look attentive and you will command attention. Among that sea of faces beyond the lectern you need every friend you can find.

So now your moment has come. Your opportunity to influence human belief and human behavior has arrived. It's also your next opportunity to establish rapport with the audience. As you scan that crowd assembled in front of you, let them know at once that *you are in charge!*

GET READY TO DELIVER

Stand and face the group for a moment before you begin, not for long, but long enough to let people settle down and anticipate your opening remark. Practice feeling them out. Soon you'll be able to calibrate the response and determine exactly when you should start.

> **SUCCESS SECRET: Don't start your speech before you reach the lectern.**

Oh-oh, look at your posture. Your toes point out, your legs are spread apart too far, and your abdomen protrudes. Let's correct that before you fall over backwards. Very slightly, point the toes in. Suck in your stomach. Keep one foot slightly, ever so slightly, behind the other. There you are. Good balance. Your weight has moved forward, and your audience has psychologically moved towards you. You now have a positive appearance! You look active! You are ready to go!

DON'T BE AFRAID TO MOVE

Personally, in public speaking I like to move about—to leave the lectern and free myself for easy expression. Be a good pupil and try it. Develop the same kind of freedom and looseness. You can do it if only you'll give it a fair try.

The great entertainer Al Jolson refused to sing unless he could be close to the people, near enough to look into their faces, and even reach out and touch them as he performed.

"Why not in speaking, too?" I asked myself. Situations do vary. It can't always be done, but oh, the fantastic results when it can be. Talk to specific individuals in the crowd. Pick the ones who will respond. You'll quickly learn to identify them.

Here's an example of how it works. Recently, I heard Somers White, one of America's top speakers, explain the complex elements that affect communication. "All of you have formed a concept of me," he said. "Each of you perceives me in a certain way as I face you from the front of the room." Continuing to speak as he moved into the audience, he said, "But watch what happens as I come closer to you." Suddenly he stopped beside a man near the back of the room. "Sir," he asked, "do you still perceive me as the same person? Am I different from the man you looked at a few moments ago?" Because of his mobility, the man easily demonstrated his thesis.

An extreme example, you are saying. Not so, not at all. I seldom make a speech without asking my audience to participate with me. They frequently help me to clinch my point, and it happens because I am near them. I like the method so well that I feel like singing "Don't Fence Me In."

But there are three other reasons for staying loose on the platform and avoiding the confinement of a lectern:

1. You remove an artificial barrier.
2. It helps you to hold attention.
3. You can move about for special effect.

Standing behind a lectern or a table automatically separates you from the audience, an undesirable relationship. If you are also framed inside a proscenium enclosure, the psychological handicap is increased. I admit there are times when a speaker cannot avoid a formal lectern, but do it when you can. It will enhance your persuasive success.

Freedom of movement helps you gain and hold attention. Learn from the techniques of a television director. How long does he leave a camera at a fixed distance or with one background? Very briefly. Lenses and cameras are altered and alternated every few seconds.

"Zoom in on one for a closeup."

"Cut one; take it two."

As each change is made, there is action and a brand-new background for the viewer to see. By moving about in front of your audience, and even in the aisles among them, you create the same kind of animation. You generate interest, hold attention, and relax both yourself and your listeners.

You can also use movement for special effects like transition or credibility. By walking to one side you actually indent a paragraph for your listeners. Let's imagine you have just finished discussing how the cost of crude oil has raised the price of gasoline. You want to persuade your audience that extravagant driving habits are also a cause. Move a few paces to the right or left as you say, "The second major reason why gasoline prices are high comes right out of our own garages. It's our wasteful use of cars for unnecessary driving."

Look what you accomplished: You have just carried your audience gracefully into a brand new topic.

SUCCESS SECRET: Always step off with the foot on the side toward which you are moving. Right to right. Left to left.

Another special effect: Movement is a persuasive device. Now imagine in your speech that you are saying, "Our company is a socially responsible corporation that cares about people." When you make that statement, would you step backward or lean away from the audience? Of course you wouldn't! That would be ludicrous and inconsistent. Instead, lean slightly forward or actually advance a step or two toward the people. If you are sitting at a meeting, lean forward as you make the statement. Simultaneously sharpen your eye contact. Then feel the surging credibility and empathy that return to you. You are like a confident prize fighter moving aggressively toward his opponent with a winner's stance and a victor's expression.

Is there ever a time when a speaker might retreat from his audience or lean away for psychological impact? Of course he might, when he discredits a fact, advises caution, or takes a negative stand on the truth or falsity of a statement.

I hope you are sufficiently intrigued so you will want to try this *open country* approach to delivery. If so, remember this success secret.

> **SUCCESS SECRET: When you leave the lectern, move with a purpose, but don't pace the room like a caged lion.**

PERSUADE WITH YOUR ARMS AND FACE

Whether you are at the lectern or in the aisle, most body messages are suggested or transmitted in exactly the same way. The body should be relaxed, but not flabby; firm, but not stiff.

> **SUCCESS SECRET: Don't let tension cramp your legs. It will creep all the way up your body, contaminate your muscles, and damage your style.**

Learn the Language of Little Kids

Because little children are nearly always relaxed, this is a good time to bring them into the monologue. You can learn magic moves from little kids. They are a whole textbook of information on body language. Emulate them. Their gestures are natural, varied, and communicative. You can literally hear a child talk with hands, shoulders, and eyes.

"I don't know why I did it." Watch the youngster's shoulders rise, his outstretched palms move upward. His eyebrows are lifted, and the lower lip protrudes.

Perplexity shows on a youngster's face long before the words, "I don't understand," form on his lips.

"He's over there, Mommy." A finger points with graceful eloquence.

Little hands divide unseen space. They create a perfect sphere. They offer with palms outstretched and they reject with vigorous thrust away.

Repair Your Body Skills

All of these communicative skills you also once possessed—until one day you looked at your hands, not as eloquent spokesmen, but as awkward appendages that retreated into the nearest pocket. From then on your arms became rusty gates.

Hands, arms, shoulders, and face can regain their former skill of expression. They can become as gracefully automative and as fluent as they ever were before. Study the child; observe trained performers as well; and use the Skill Builders to develop your body language to its fullest potential.

SUCCESS SECRET: Body language conveys 40 percent of your communication message.

That fact should motivate you to try harder. Here are some rules to help you.

Eight Rules for Natural Gestures

1. Don't use the same gesture over and over again.
2. Don't gesture continuously like the endless turning of a windmill.
3. Make your movements consistent with the words you are saying.
4. Make your gestures fit the environment and the size of your audience. Generally, use compact gestures for small groups and broader, more expansive movements for large audiences.
5. Don't terminate a gesture at the halfway mark. Complete it.
6. If you are positive of a fact, move forward as you say it; if doubtful, lean backward.
7. The arms, shoulders, and face should work in concert to communicate and persuade.
8. Strive for naturalness. Don't let your gestures call attention to themselves.

Now, let's use the Skill Builders for some fun-to-do exercises.

LET'S PRACTICE

Skill Builders

Stand several feet away from a mirror, preferably full-length. Imagine you are looking out at an audience.

1. Keep eye contact sharp. Actually see the audience in front of you. Develop a smooth head movement. Don't swing your head back and forth like a person watching a tennis match. Look to the right. Actually *see* a person out there.

Move back to the middle, then part way back to the right. Now gradually work your way to the left. Avoid rapid, jerky movements. Don't neglect any part of the audience. In every part of the room, imagine there is a SPECIFIC person that you are talking to. Then, when you get into a real, live situation you will actually discover that there are people out there to make contact with.

2. Ever so slightly, lean forward and say, "Sir, I'm talking to you." Now, repeat the expression and step toward the mirror. Purposely put tension in your voice and let your finger come up to point.

3. Leaning slightly backward as you talk, say, "I'm really not sure about this." Repeat the words, actually taking a step or two backward. Keep trying the exercise until you feel comfortable with it.

4. Step to the left. (Remember to lead off with the left foot.) Return to your original position and do it again, this time saying, "Let's look at the other side of this question." Repeat the exercise, using only one hand.

5. Using both hands, with the palms upward, say, "I want you to accept this idea." Be sure the gesture comes up naturally. Repeat the exercise, using only one hand.

6. Turning your palms downward and pushing away from the body, say, "I don't want any part of it!" Repeat the exercise using only one hand. (Notice how the body tends to move away from the mirror as you make these negative statements.)

7. On your own, make up two opposite, contrasting ideas, and demonstrate them with your hands. For example, show how some people advocate rationing as a way to curtail gasoline consumption while others believe in letting high prices control purchases.

8. Make up appropriate gestures for "It was a fish this long." "I have a box about eight inches high and, oh, probably about this long." "You can't force that theory on me!"

9. Move close to the mirror and make faces showing anger, perplexity, disbelief, cynicism, joy, enthusiasm, and disappointment.

10. With strong, inward feeling say, "I really couldn't care less about what you think!" Try to use the face, the arms, and shoulders in a concert of body expression, even exaggerating slightly for maximum effect.

11. At night before you go to sleep, picture yourself performing on the platform. Visualize your body making smooth, appropriate gestures to augment statements you create as you lie in bed.

PRESS THE MAGIC-MEMORY STAMP

The body communicates 40 percent of your message.

Look alert in sight of your audience, even when you are not speaking.

Your approach to the platform is a critical moment in persuasion. It presets the way people perceive you as a person and predetermines in part your eventual effectiveness.

Learn to wander away from the lectern for greatest effectiveness.

Gestures should supplement your ideas. Be natural, complete, and varied.

Daily practice improves body messages and encourages the body to perform automatically in real speaking situations.

A LOOK AHEAD

Illustrations, quotations, comparisons, and statistics are the stuff from which speeches are made. People often say to me, "I can't make a speech because I don't know what to talk about." We'll examine that problem in the next chapter. We'll help you to discover subjects for your persuasive talks.

Finding a topic is much easier if you have an abundance of material standing by to suggest ideas to you. The secret of finding material is also revealed in the next chapter along with several pages of illustrations and quotations that can become your starter set of persuasive support material. Once you begin your collection, it will grow at a steady rate, especially after you become aware of what to look for, where to find it, and how to file it for easy retrieval.

Let's turn the page for the next secrets of persuasion.

chapter 7

Turn Your Beliefs into Speeches

"What shall I talk about?"

"I can't think of a thing to say."

Sound familiar? Are these things that have bothered you? If so, fear not, because you are in the majority. Part of the problem may be a subconscious impediment—the *fear complex* I discussed in Chapter 1. Or it may only be that you haven't appraised your potential for uncovering speech topics. Most people are pleasantly surprised to discover they are full of subjects just waiting to be brought to the surface. *What to talk about* is nowhere near as perplexing as you think.

THAW OUT YOUR FEAR

If the problem is a self-conscious feeling that what you have to say is not important, forget it. Every person has a speech inside—as well as the ability to dredge it up, develop it, and deliver it with persuasive effectiveness.

Here is a success example: Martha Jurgenson was a junior in high school when I invited her to prepare an oration for interscholastic competition. Her reaction was extreme, almost hysterical.

"Who would ever listen to *me?*" she shrieked. But I persisted in my persuasion until Martha finally agreed to participate. Because she was already in my speech class, I could easily help her to choose and develop her topic.

Martha's first entry into contest speaking ended in near disaster. She was ranked tenth out of ten, *but she did not quit.* Each time she appeared in subsequent tournaments she tried harder and improved her ratings. Soon she was defeating seasoned high school speakers. It was like a miracle that she won the state contest only four and a half months after her first discouraging appearance.

Near the end of Martha's college career, almost six years later, she won the first-place trophy in a national intercollegiate oratory contest. (Her coach in those years was George McGovern, candidate for the United States Presidency in 1976.)

> **SUCCESS SECRET: Many good speeches have been permanently frozen in the ice of personal fear.**

HOW TO UNLOCK YOUR SPEECH SUBJECTS

Your Interests and Information are Primary

A person's beliefs and background will nearly always yield a list of worthwhile speech topics. The places one visits and the books and articles one reads are rich areas in which to search for treasures.

Example

I was sent to Africa and to Central America to prepare a slide/cassette tape for an agency in Washington, D.C. I returned with a full reservoir of material that later became a deep source of speech ideas. In their broad, unrefined form, the subjects included

International poverty
The value of cooperative ventures in developing nations
Appreciation for the American free-choice system

Helpful tips for recording adventures on tape
and film

The need to stay trim and fit if one is to enjoy
exciting adventures

All these general topics evolved into speeches that I
delivered after returning home.

Don't Overlook Your Audience's Interests

Often your audience's needs and interests will dictate
your speech topic. If your background and their interests
coincide, you will be able to create a speech that fits the
occasion perfectly. But do not commit yourself to speak on
subjects that are outside the scope of your knowledge and
experience.

Example

My brother, Dr. John E. Turner, a well-known political
science professor at the University of Minnesota,
speaks often and authoritatively about China, the
Soviet Union, and Great Britain. He has visited all
these countries frequently and has written books
about two of them. On the other hand, the subjects I
talk about are far-removed from John's background.
Neither of us has ever crossed the border into the
other's territory.

**SUCCESS SECRET: If you don't know more about
the subject than your audience does, you are probably
standing on thin ice.**

NARROW YOUR SUBJECT

Henry Ford once recommended that big jobs be broken into little tasks so that we can "get our arms around
them." Speech topics are the same way. No one should ever
try to make a persuasive speech about the general subject

of *health.* Instead, establish a specific purpose or aim regarding health. What do you want to accomplish? What do you want people to believe? When you realize that *what you believe* and *what you want the audience to believe are the same thing,* then you are on the way to successful personal persuasion. I like to think of pouring my general speech subject into a *separator funnel.* It has two stages. Phase I filters out the specific conclusion I want to sell. Phase II isolates (at least in a preliminary fashion) the main reasons that make my conclusion believable. The process is actually an application of Henry Ford's suggestion that the task be broken into small bits so that I can handle it.

> *Example*
>
> A moment ago I mentioned a speech on health that germinated in connection with my trip to Africa. I knew that I wanted to talk about health, so I ran that general topic through Phase I of the separator funnel. Whenever I found a spare moment, I let it process, and I always wrote down the results, even if they seemed far removed from anything I might use.
>
> Eventually, the conclusion crystallized: "One should stay in shape to enjoy exciting experiences." In the development process I was able to give the speech universal appeal by eliminating the restriction of talking only about an overseas excursion. As I moved into Phase II of the separator funnel, the topic acquired even broader audience appeal as segments of the conclusion began to present themselves. Here are a few of the items I eventually selected for my speech:
>
> 1. I feared I was not in good condition for the photo assignment. (This served as an audience penetration point for my speech.)
> 2. A regular program of health improvement can be enjoyable.
> 3. A healthy body causes a person to reach out for fun and equips one to meet emergencies.

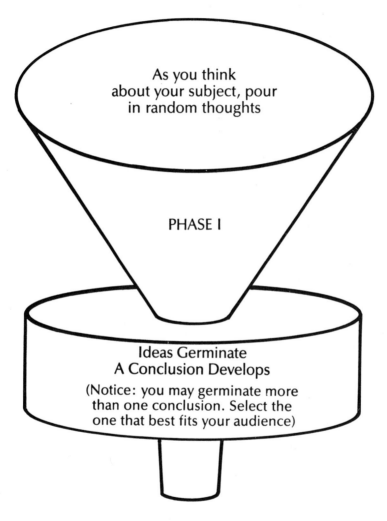

As you think
about your subject, pour
in random thoughts

PHASE I

Ideas Germinate
A Conclusion Develops

(Notice: you may germinate more
than one conclusion. Select the
one that best fits your audience)

A conclusion comes
through with surprising
ease.

Art by Roger Jensen

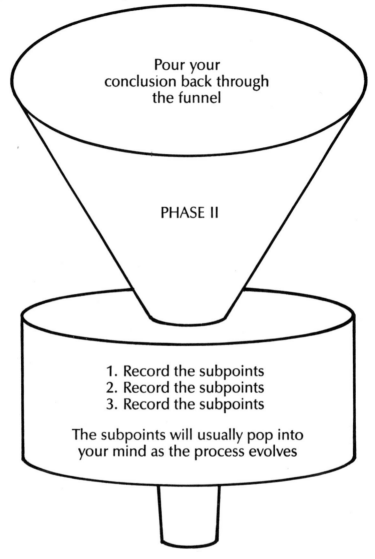

Pour your
conclusion back through
the funnel

PHASE II

1. Record the subpoints
2. Record the subpoints
3. Record the subpoints

The subpoints will usually pop into
your mind as the process evolves

Support material will flow from
the funnel as your mind continues
to process the subject. When a
story, example, quotation, or statistical
item occurs to you, *write it down.*

Art by Roger Jensen

This is not the finished speech. It is only a threshold from which to proceed towards the final product. The funnel is a gimmick that suggests speech possibilities. It lets one know whether or not there might be sufficient meat to warrant continuation of the development process.

By feeding and refeeding the data into this imaginary funnel, ideas appear as if by magic. The support material itself often flows out of the funnel spout. For instance, one of the most energetic, fun-filled people I encountered on my African trip was a seventy-six-year-old woman who was prowling about inside the Great Pyramid outside Cairo. Her effervescent activities appeared prominently as an illustration in my speech. So did several quotations from my physician who had helped me prepare for the trip. So did the negative example of the fifty-year-old man, tired and cranky, who should have stayed in Iowa and rocked on his patio. He wasn't prepared to enjoy "exciting experiences."

Skill Builder

Make a list of subjects that interest you. For example:

safety	investing
democratic choice	problem solving
people	money management
elements of success	community service
cooperation	good government

Select your favorite topic from the list and run it through the separator funnel. Write down the things that flow out. You'll soon realize whether or not you have a background on the subject and whether or not there is sufficient flow to justify further effort. Be sure to write down the results. Try to crystallize an idea into a firm premise that you believe in and that you can persuade an audience to accept.

After a few days on the project you will probably be amazed at how far you have traveled down the road to a complete speech. These results usually occur:

1. The statement of belief (your premise) takes shape.
2. Your main support statements often appear. (You can encourage this step by asking *why* and *how* questions about your belief. *Why* should I get in condition? *How* should I get in condition?)
3. Some of the support material (illustrations, quotations, and statistics) will present themselves.

Indeed, *sufficient* support material is probably all that you lack after you complete Phase II of the separation funnel. We are ready to deal with that project now.

ADD STRENGTH TO YOUR PERSUASION

Support material usually includes illustrations, comparisons, quotations, and statistics. Generous use of these tools is a requisite for persuasion. They will build muscles within your speech. Particularly at this time, I want to discuss how to use illustrations and start your collection of persuasive stories and quotations. *Deadly* and *dull* are frightening words that plague every speaker who avoids using stories. If you would acquire the magic power of personal persuasion, remember that *a story is worth two thousand words*—and it might be the most important part .of your speech.

Here's an example: Once I returned to a city in Iowa where I had made a speech many years earlier. While waiting for the program to begin, a member of the audience said to me, "I remember the last time you were here. You talked about flying over New York and seeing the Statue of Liberty."

Although flattered that the listener had remembered the incident, I hoped that my flying experience was not the only thing he could recall. By probing with a few questions, I discovered that he retained the gist of the entire speech. Seven years had elapsed; yet, an idea remained fresh and memorable *because I told an interesting story about a flight over a historic monument.*

A drab presentation of expository facts usually bores the audience, no matter how well the facts are phrased or how tightly they are laced together. At a large corporate meeting, I heard a speaker present superior material—fact piled upon fact, each illustrated with excellent visual charts projected on a giant screen. The speaker was competent; the pictures were dramatic; but these were not enough. The speech needed room to breathe—personal examples, stories, anecdotes. Soon members of the audience began to leave. At the close of the fifty-minute monologue, over half of the people—discourteous though they may have been—had left the auditorium. Most of those who remained were paralyzed with drowsiness.

Learn the lesson and learn it well: A story here, an example there, make all the difference in the world. They give magic warmth to your materials; they hold attention; they cause people to remember—*and to believe*—what you are saying. After all, that's what personal persuasion is all about.

The process is simple: State the point you want to make. Explain it (that's always a necessary step); then tell the perfect story that makes your point believable, or give a real live example of where it happened, how someone else discovered and used this truth, and so forth.

SUCCESS SECRET: Carefully illustrating your material with well-chosen examples and stories adds magic power to personal persuasion.

Three questions need to be answered:

1. How should you use examples, stories, and illustrations?
2. Where can you find good stories?
3. How should you catalog this material?

I'll answer these questions and then provide you with a good starter set of illustrations for your own *personal persuasion collection*. In general, an illustration is an example or a clarifying story. It often, but not always, has people or animals playing key roles. It may have a simple plot. Sometimes it's called a vignette or a *slice of life*.

A humorous story can do everything an illustration does. In addition, however, it can serve as a breather in the speech or an attention-getter whose primary purpose is *not* persuading but merely breaking the action and giving the audience a lighter moment. (You'll learn more about humor in the next chapter.)

HOW TO USE STORIES

Now let's answer the first question: How should you use examples?

You have often heard people say, "For instance..." These are magic words, arrows that point toward a clarifying story. And that's really all there is to the process. Make a statement, explain it, and give a "for instance."

Here is a "for instance" for the statement I have just made—a support chain, which, though simple, would give power to a speaker's statement:

Statement: To alter the organizational structure of our company is undesirable at this time.

Principle: We often create our own problems.

Clarification: It frequently is better to leave a working situation alone than to completely overhaul it. When one's life, one's job, and one's family are galloping along smoothly, why should we disrupt the quiet of well-meshed gears?

Quotation: As the old saying goes, "If it ain't broke, don't fix it."

Example: For instance: Our bread toaster was working fine. My wife had not complained about it. The machine never burned the bread. It readily responded to the "darkness" control. But somehow I convinced myself that it ought to be doing a better job, so I proceeded to overhaul it. I stripped it completely and expertly reassembled it. The toaster doesn't work any better nor, I admit, is it *any less* efficient than before. But in the overhauling process, I lost a small piece of spring steel that locks one of the controls in place. I'll never find it and I can't locate a new one; so the control just hangs there waiting to fall off every time the toaster is touched.

Restatement: "If it ain't broke, don't fix it." It is often better to leave a working machine alone. We must not re-organize our company at this time.

One does not need to be profound to be effective. There's magic power in the stories you choose and use.

WHERE TO LOOK FOR ILLUSTRATIONS

Let's turn now to the second question: Where can you find good stories?

Like trees in the great Northwest, good stories flourish everywhere. I find them in people—in their lives, in their reactions, in the things that happen to them.

I find analogies (illustrations built on similarities) in animals. A peculiar weakness of Old Roy, the bull dog I owned when I was a child, provided me with an illustration that carries the major portion of a goal-setting speech that I frequently present to management groups. Roy liked to chase rabbits. As he raced across the prairie in pursuit of his prey, a second rabbit often crossed between them. Roy would hesitate, uncertain about which animal to run after. By the time he decided, both rabbits had disappeared.

Books and magazines yield excellent stories. The Bible is loaded with examples that relate directly to management and scores of other subjects. One of the great precedents for *delegation* comes directly from the story of Moses (Exodus 18:17-22).

Other speakers provide good illustrations. Never steal another person's speech, but you can borrow the stories used as illustrations. These are usually in the *public domain;* if not, giving credit to the source even as you speak is adequate compensation for their use.

> **SUCCESS SECRET: Seek and you will find. If you wish to locate good stories, you'll discover them with magic ease.**

HOW TO KEEP TRACK OF YOUR STORIES

Let's answer the hardest and final question: How should you catalog your materials?

Complex methods of cataloging are generally to be avoided. If the task becomes onerous, you'll not enjoy doing it and you probably won't maintain your file. Why commit yourself to an impossible task that merely builds stress and creates frustration?

> **SUCCESS SECRET: Whatever works best for you is the filing system you ought to use.**

There is, of course, a complex method for filing material if that's what you need, but I've known only one or two people who ever used it. It's like the Dewey Decimal System for cataloging library books. The method virtually dictates that each illustration be typed on a separate index card. You must invent the major classes (probably ten or less) that embrace all of your material. Each class is then given a number that never changes. Subsequently, each category is divided and subdivided as many times as necessary, and a standard number is assigned to every level.

If the classifying is accomplished logically, the system is efficient. Whenever one needs a story to support a specific point, the numbering system leads directly to the desired item. Because very few people need a method this complex, I'll spend no more time on it. If you desire to learn more about it, I recommend that you study the Dewey Decimal method at your local library and adapt its principles for your cataloging method.

> **SUCCESS SECRET: The best rule for most people is "keep it simple."**

To initiate a simple, yet effective method for arranging your illustrations, decide whether you prefer using index cards or a notebook. Cards are portable and easy to store. As you are preparing a speech, they can be arranged and rearranged in a changing order. Notebooks are easy to maintain. One seldom misplaces stories that have been typed on a page and filed in a three-ring binder.

I have tried both systems. The notebook method works best for me. I am familiar with most of my illustrations because I encounter them often while thumbing through the pages in search of support. Years ago, when I was using the index-card system, I somehow did not receive this frequent exposure. As a result, I often forgot that certain stories were in my file *even though they were adequately cataloged*. For me it is the mere physical act of paging through my notebook that makes the difference. A little later I shall discuss this phenomenon with you again.

Skill Builders

Open your notebook or card file and read through the stories you have collected. You will see that each illustration tends to fit under a *classifying word.* Some of these words are: leadership, organization, accomplishment, reward, and trust. These groups become your tentative categories. If you find that the number of classes is growing too rapidly, see if you can combine some of them into broader, more general terms.

Write the classifying word in the margin to the left of the story in your notebook or on top of the index card in your file. (Use pencil. You may want to change it.)

If you are using an index-card system, group the cards into their assigned categories by inserting spacers in your card box. This obviously establishes a section for each category.

In the notebook method, some people prefer to *group all stories of one category on a single page.* I don't. I use the "run-on" method; that is, when I discover a new story, I type it or write it immediately after the prior entry in the notebook. I write the classifying word in the margin. Retrieving is easy. I merely skim the marginal notes, picking out all the items included in a specific category.

As you collect more and more material, you will find subclasses developing. Merely write the subclass word in the margin of the notebook or at the top of the index card.

The notebook method has two distinct advantages:

1. It is simple but not haphazard. (I can retrieve rapidly.)
2. The system provides frequent exposure to all your material. Each time you search for illustrations to magnify your persuasive power, your eyes will scan every item that you have saved. It's a subliminal touch, but an effective one. *I truly believe that ad-libbing the final speech is made easier because of this familiarity.*

To cross-reference your material within the catalog system is a simple process. Assume you are using the card file system and that you have a story on *sharing*. Obviously it will be filed in that category, but it also fits in the *leadership* section. Merely insert a card in the leadership category that says: "See also: sharing—story about the boss who gave bonus."

If you use the notebook method,your story is labeled "sharing." In the margin, under sharing, write "leadership" and the note: "See also: sharing—story about the boss who gave bonus.

Here is a time and space saver: Don't write out your illustrations in full. Just sketch the elements of the story; then, when you need to use the illustration, recreate its components in an interesting style. This practice has several advantages:

1. It conserves time and space.
2. It develops your creative intelligence.
3. It helps you adapt the story to a specific audience (such as attorneys, corporate executives, farmers, or sales people) by using their terminology and background in the example.
4. It develops your magic power to ad-lib.

PRESS THE MAGIC-MEMORY STAMP

Speeches without illustrations are deadly and dull. A story is worth two thousand words.

Examples give magic warmth to the speech material. They cause people to remember; they create belief.

State your point, explain it, then add the perfect story to complete the persuasion process.

Good illustrations are all around us waiting to be collected.

Develop a simple, usable system for classifying your materials.

Don't write out the details of your illustration. Include only the essential elements of your stories.

START YOUR OWN SPEECH FILE

Would you like a "starter set" of stories? I'm going to give you some for your own collection. I have classified some of the early stories to show how it is done. (The classification words precede each story.) You should do the rest on your own for practice and experience.

SUCCESS SECRET: Learn the value of illustrations. Use them. Let them increase your magic power.

HERE IS YOUR BONUS SET OF MAGIC STORIES

Dedication

Jethro, Moses' father-in-law, saw Moses staggering under the same problem that has killed many modern executives. All by himself, Moses was trying to perform the impossible task of judging and supervising his people. Jethro came to Moses and said, "The thing you are doing is not good. You will surely wear away, both you and these people who are with you; for this thing is too heavy for you; you are not able to perform it by yourself." The father-in-law then counseled Moses on how to solve the problem, "...you shall select from all the people, able men to be rulers of thousands, and rulers of hundreds, rulers of fifties and rulers of tens. Let them judge the people at all seasons. Every great matter they shall bring to you, every small matter they shall judge; so, it will be easier for you and they will bear the burden with you."

Moses listened to the words of his father-in-law and did all that he said. He chose...able men out of all Israel and made them heads over the people...and they judged the people at all seasons. The hard causes they brought to Moses, but every small matter they judged themselves." (Exodus 18:17–22 Paraphrased and quoted from the King James version.)

Goals

Chief Justice Holmes entered Pennsylvania Station unaware that he had misplaced his ticket until the last minute. He made a quick but methodical search through his coat and his briefcase. The trainmaster, recognizing both the man and his plight, reassured the judge. "Justice Holmes," he said, "you can board without your ticket. You'll probably find it later."

Holmes quickly replied, "I don't think you understand my problem, Sir. If I don't find the ticket, I don't know where I'm going."

Interpersonal Dependence

Every morning on his way to the factory, a worker passed by a jewelry store. Invariably he stopped, took out an old pocket watch, and set the hands by a huge clock in the window.

One morning the jeweler confronted him. "Sir," he said, "for a long time I've been watching you set your watch by my clock. Why do you do that?"

The man motioned towards the factory at the end of the street. "I work down there," he said. "Part of my job is to blow the whistle. I have to be sure I blow it on time."

The jeweler grinned, then broke into hearty laughter. "Mister," he said, "that's the funniest thing I've ever heard. Every day for a long time I've been setting my clock by that whistle."

Monotony

According to Greek mythology, Sisyphus, a cruel King of Corinth, was sentenced for his heinous crimes. As punishment he was required each morning to push a giant boulder up a hill. It took him all day to reach the summit; then, at night, he was required to push the stone off its resting place and let it roll down the hill to its starting point. Day after day, year after year, he inched the stone up the hillside and each night he let it roll down again. How many find that their jobs become this kind of monotonous exercise. The myth of the cruel king was the Greek concept of Hell.

Motivation: External Pressure

Percy is a robot. Percy is fiction. But Percy is a very effective fictitious robot. On the back of this lifelike metal man is a row of keys or buttons, each clearly marked with the name of a common task, such as mow the lawn, wash the dishes, type the letter. Percy quickly responds to whatever key is depressed. As soon as each task is completed, however, the robot stands—or sits— until another button has been pushed. And if no one is around to put him back in motion, Percy doesn't do anything.

Motivation: Internal Initiative

At a management school session on goal setting, the instructor drew a sketch of a large wire cage. In one end he placed a dozing white rat. At the other end he drew a huge block of cheese. In the middle of the cage he sketched a strong metal gate separating the rat from the cheese.

"In due time," the instructor said, "this rat awakens and moves to the center of the cage where, quite by accident, he trips the lever that opens the gate. The rat enters the other compartment and eats some of the cheese; then he returns to his side of the cage, and the gate automatically snaps shut. But in an hour or two, the rat returns to search again for the lever. When he steps on it, the gate obediently drops, the rat eats, and returns once more to his nest." The teacher let his story soak in before asking the class, "What motivated that rat?" One young man in the group immediately raised his hand. "I know, Sir. It was the cheese."

A sly grin slowly spread over the instructor's face. He shook his head back and forth. "No way," he drawled. "The motivation was the hunger inside the beast."

Performance Appraisal

A young man entered a neighborhood drugstore and asked if he might use the telephone. The proprietor granted his request; then, without meaning to eavesdrop, overheard the one-sided conversation.

"Hello," the young man said. "Is this Anderson's Market?" Then, after a pause, "Do you have an opening for a stockboy? What? You already have one? Well, is he doing a good job for you? He's great? Okay. Thank you."

The druggist was impressed with the young man's approach. "Say there, Son," he said, "I didn't mean to listen to your conversation, but I'm looking for a good man like you. How would you like to work in my drugstore?"

"Gee, thanks," the man replied, "but I already have a job at Anderson's. I was just checking to see if I'm doing okay."

Productivity

A psychologist engaged an expert woodsman to help him with a production experiment. The man, who habitually felled scores of trees every day, was sent into the forest with only one instruction: "Spend the day swinging at trees with the blunt side of your ax." Before noon he emerged from the woods and quit the job. When asked why he was leaving, the woodsman answered, "I have to see the chips fly."

Service

While cleaning a closet, a woman discovered a shoe repair ticket that was more than five years old. Apparently she had never returned to pick up her merchandise. One day she dropped in at the shop and presented the ticket to a clerk, who immediately retreated to the back of the store. In a few moments he returned and said, "I'm so sorry, Ma'am, but your shoes won't be ready until Tuesday."

Responsibility

Once there was an old professor whose wisdom was recognized throughout the land. A young college boy decided he would test, and try to confuse, this learned man. He thought, *I shall catch a bird and approach the professor holding the bird behind my back. I will then ask him what I hold in my hand. Because he is wise, he shall say,* "It is a bird." *Then I will ask whether the bird is dead or alive. If he says,* "Dead," *I shall release it and let it fly away. If he says,* "Alive," *I'll crush the bird between my fingers.*

Armed with this dilemma, the young man approached the sage. "Tell me, Sir, what do I have in my hand?"

"It is a bird," the wise man answered promptly.

"Is it dead or is it alive?" the young man asked.

The old man pondered for a moment, then answered sadly, "My Son, the answer to that question is in your hands."

Beginning now, classify the remaining stories and quotations in your starter set.

An old Chinese legend: A sculptor creates two clay statues. One of them is I; one of them is you. While the clay is still wet, he destroys both statues by mixing the clay together and then reshaping them into two fresh clay statues. But an interaction occurs that can never be altered: A little bit of *you* has become a little bit of *me*, and a little bit of *me* has become a little bit of *you*—and it can never be changed.

A lumber company hired a strapping young fellow to cut timber in the woods. On the first morning the young man, with his ax across his broad shoulders, went out to fell trees. The first day he cut 100. The next day he cut 120, and the third day, 125. On the fourth day his production began to fall off. At the end of two weeks, he was cutting only 80 trees a day. The foreman called him in and said, "John, I want to talk about your job. The first day you were here—when we were just breaking you in—you knocked down a hundred trees. Now you are cutting only 80 a day. What's the problem?" The young man gave the foreman a very unusual answer; yet, one that is typical in all production effort. "Yes Sir," he said, "I know I'm falling behind, but I'm working harder than I ever did. In fact, I'm working so hard I haven't even had time to sharpen my ax."

In an old fable, a bird meets a fisherman who has a can of worms. The bird asks for one worm.

"Sure," the fisherman said. "All I ask in return is one of your feathers."

A feather for a worm seemed reasonable, so the bird made the exchange. The next day the bird was hungry again. Weighing the inconvenience of searching for food against the expedience of trading another of his feathers to the fisherman, he decided in favor of expediency. After a few days, the bird had traded away so many feathers he could no longer fly; so each day he walked to the fisherman's shack to receive a worm. Finally, all of his feathers were gone. At this point, the fisherman picked up the fat naked bird and cooked him for dinner.

Tom, Dick, and Harry—three pigs from the same litter—were distinguished guests at the State Fair. Each had been scientifically fed. Tom was raised on balanced rations, a dietary course in which he was permitted to balance his meals according to his own appetite. In six months, he gained 94 pounds and was worth less than the feed he had eaten. Dick ate the same scientifically balanced ration, but was also given some alfalfa each day to nose and eat between meals. He gained 200 pounds in six months and earned a fine profit. Harry was fed the same as Tom plus the alfalfa that Dick received. He also had an open range where he was allowed to roam and root in nearby fields. He gained 300 pounds in six months.

In these days of rapid learning, there is need for more than spoon-fed static information. Gates must be opened through which we can move to satisfy our intellectual appetites and enrich the storehouse of our minds.

The rhinoceros is a fairly stupid animal and a ferocious sight. He also has a unique characteristic: He is apt to charge full steam at his enemies; then, in the middle of the charge, he seems to forget what he is doing. He stops abruptly in the middle of the effort and goes away by himself to graze.

A wise supervisor described the proper way to direct people: "When you want someone to learn a new skill and to see your point of view, don't stand across the room and shout instructions at him. Don't call him a dummy if he doesn't seem to understand at once. Don't order him to begin working at the job without proper background. Instead, start where he is and work from that position. Mentally speaking, *you go to where he is standing, take him by the hand, and guide him to where you want him to be.* That's the only way to teach new skills to either a child or an adult."

Enthusiasm can often compensate for luxury. Necessity can often be the mother of invention. Years ago before kids had ever heard of football scholarships or high-priced baseball players, they rolled string into a tight ball and made a casing by wrapping many layers of electrician's tape on the outside. Sometimes an old stick or a log became the baseball bat; yet, lack of equipment did not diminish the excitement of the game. The inability to buy high-priced fishing gear did not curtail the zeal for fishing. A willow switch cut along the bank of a stream served very well as a pole; a pin tied to one end of a piece of string often sufficed for a hook. Perhaps this crude equipment would not have captured a six-pound walleye, but it snagged some awfully good bullheads and provided hundreds of relaxing hours.

During the Depression, 200 young people attended a camp in the Black Hills of South Dakota. On the second day, a young man named Jim broke out with a serious case of poison ivy. Because he failed to respond to usual remedies, the camp nurse transported him to a hospital in Rapid City. But Jim had no money for his medical bills. A young leader in the camp summoned everyone to a meeting and made an unusual suggestion: "Let's close the camp store, pool all our spending money, and pay Jim's hospital bill." The young people responded with an enthusiastic cheer. Although few had more than twenty-five cents to contribute, every nickel was dropped into the hat. The camp store, with its goodies of candy and pop, was closed for the duration of the camp. Years later, one of the people (now a prominent businessman) recalled, "I'm sure my tax dollars have gone to take care of a great many people in need, but I'm equally sure that I have never felt the power of giving as strongly as I did that week in South Dakota."

If we have interest in a task, we usually have the energy to carry it out. A man may be lazy on the job but will hunt diligently for antelope in the mountains. A factory worker may not like to get up in the morning for work but will rise willingly on Saturday, drive a hundred miles, and fish for hours through a hole in the ice during a blinding snowstorm. Enthusiasm creates energy. Distaste for a job dries it up.

A few years ago a man walked across the United States. The media interviewed him. A reporter asked, "Which gave you more trouble, rivers or mountains?"

"Neither one," the man replied. "It was the sand in my shoes." The nitty-gritty often creates more difficulty than some of the big things in life.

A college professor with a high energy level worked hard, slept little, and played not at all. Because he never seemed to relax, his wife became concerned and finally persuaded him to see a physician. Meanwhile, she told the doctor confidentially about her concerns. When the professor went for his examination, he was given more of an interview than an inspection.

"You are your own biggest enemy, Professor," the doctor said. "You absolutely have to learn how to slow down."

The professor replied, "I know I go fast, but it's the way I'm built. I can't help it."

"Then you'd better try," the doctor said. "I'm going to prescribe a hobby for you. Now don't feel like a sissy because I ask you to try this—I want you to learn how to make hooked rugs. I think you'll enjoy it and I think it will be good for you to work with your hands."

When the professor returned to his home, he explained to his wife what the doctor had prescribed. He didn't know it, but it was really her prescription. Together they went to a shopping center and bought all of the equipment that he would need for his hobby.

That night the professor stayed up until 2:00 A.M. reading the directions and learning the technique.

Within two weeks he had made so many hooked rugs that there were few places left in the house to scatter them. He still maintained his heavy schedule at the college but reduced his sleeping hours so that he could manufacture more rugs.

For some, *work* is a way of life, and inescapable burnout lies at the end of the tunnel.

A large northern pike was placed in one side of an aquarium. A host of minnows occupied the other side, separated from the pike by a glass partition. The pike often dived at the minnows only to bruise his nose on the glass. Each time he attempted to snap at one of the small fish, he hurt himself again. Eventually he quit trying. Satisfied that he was conditioned to leave the fish alone, a psychologist removed the glass partition. From then on, the minnows swam about unmolested in the water. Even though hungry, the pike never ate a minnow again.

A salesman sat in the office of a New England businessman. To make conversation, he pointed to a photo on the businessman's desk. "Is that a picture of your father?" he asked.

"Nope," the businessman replied. "That's a man I used to work for. Meanest fellow I ever knew. I keep the picture around to remind myself to stay on the ball in case I'd end up working for him again."

Several young boys were playing on a football field after a light snow had fallen. They competed to see who could make the straightest tracks across the field. One boy invariably walked a straighter course than all the rest. They begged him to tell them how he did it. "It's easy," he proclaimed. "Just pick a spot on the other side and walk straight to it."

Water boils at 212 degrees. One degree less can stop a turbine, shutting down an entire industry. That extra tiny bit of energy can score a touchdown in the closing seconds of a football game. That *little bit more* can mean the difference between success and failure.

A middle-aged educator accepted the presidency of a small dilapidated college in a remote Rocky Mountain valley. Two worn-out buildings and one new one, half finished, constituted the campus. "We'll remake it," the new president declared. "We'll bring in faculty. We'll build an academic program, and a football team, and a debate program—and a band. There are only nine people in our band, but we'll build the best in the West."

Seven years later *a man with a dream* had assembled a faculty with a purpose. New buildings penetrated the wilderness of chico weed. The student body had grown by more than seven hundred. And his band marched in the Tournament of Roses Parade.

Listening pays dividends. A school teacher met with the president of the Board of Education to apply for a job. After the formalities of introduction, the president talked uninterrupted for nearly half an hour. Then, at the close of the monologue he said, "Mr. Swartz, we're going to hire you because you're such a good conversationalist."

A lion strolled into a clearing and emitted a mighty roar. The other animals scrambled fearfully into the forest to hide. Later a rabbit entered the clearing and released a shrill, piercing squeak. The other animals rushed into the clearing and mauled the rabbit. Never advertise unless you can deliver the goods.

In the old days a worker was usually a small cog in the wheel. Today he's fifteen holes in a computer card.

A traveler asked an airport policeman for information and received a response that was more insulting than informative. "Sir," the traveler said, "please give me your name and badge number. I'd like to mention them to your supervisor when I write about how helpful you have been."

A customer was much impressed by the good service he received at a restaurant. As he paid his check, he asked the manager how he trained his help. "I don't have to train them much," the manager replied. "I pick them that way, then I know they are sincere when they serve their customers."

Two sailors were visiting near the railing of their ship when another crew member called to them, "Man your posts! The ship is sinking!"

One of the sailors shouted back, "Let 'er sink. We don't own it."

A chairman introduced the speaker as a "self-made man." In his opening remarks the speaker acknowledged that indeed he was considered to be self-made. "But, if I had to do it over," he said, "I'd try to get a little help."

In the early days of the fast-food business, a man developed a very successful hamburger drive-in café in a small Midwestern community. To provide superior service, he hired a staff of five or six carhops to be on duty at all times. His sandwiches consistently contained a generous portion of first-grade meat. One Thanksgiving holiday the proprietor's son returned from the university where he was studying economics.

"The economy doesn't look good, Dad," the student cautioned. "We might be going into a depression. I think you should lay off one of those carhops." The father took his son's advice.

At Christmas the boy came home again, more convinced than ever that there was going to be a depression. "You'd better cut down on the hamburger," he warned.

Periodically the young student predicted a dangerous depression and each time recommended ways for his father to reduce overhead.

"Fire another carhop—use a smaller bun—put in less hamburger."

Finally, one summer day the proprietor sat on the steps of his deserted restaurant. The lot was empty; the carhops were all gone. "By golly," the father lamented, "my kid was right; there is a depression."

A new resident in a small town was getting acquainted with her next-door neighbor. "I know I am going to like your town," the new resident said, "except for your awful hardware store. I've never had such terrible service in my life."

"That's strange," the neighbor said. "The owner is a good friend of ours, and his hardware store has a reputation for giving very good service."

"Well, I wish you'd tell him what I think of his store," the neighbor insisted. "As far as I'm concerned, he runs a sloppy business."

A few days later the newcomer encountered her neighbor again. "Say," she said, "you really must have straightened out that friend of yours in the hardware store. I went there this morning, and the service was terrific. The manager even told me to let him know if he can help my husband and me with our projects. You must have really told him off."

"No, I didn't tell him off at all," the woman replied. "I merely told him that you were new in town and that you were impressed with his fine hardware store."

An old Chinese patriarch spent his lifetime amassing great wealth. On his deathbed he summoned his three sons to his side to assure them that their futures and fortunes depended on their ability to work together. Then he asked the oldest boy to bring a bundle of sticks from the nearby fireplace. The son obeyed. "I want each of you," the father said, "to break this bundle in the middle." Each tried in turn, but all of them failed. Once more the patriarch gave instructions to the oldest. "Untie the bundle, my Son. Take a stick for yourself and hand one to each of your brothers." When this was accomplished, the father said, "Each of you now try to break your stick." Of course all of them easily performed the task. "Never separate, my Sons," the father counseled. "Stick together and no one can harm you."

A truck driver came to a highway overpass that was only one or two inches lower than the top of his load. His vehicle, of course, could not go through. Because the driver was blocking the roadway, a crowd of impatient motorists soon assembled, many of them with their horns blaring. Others presented helpful ideas on how to solve the problem. Taking an alternate route seemed sensible enough, except that the other road was gravel-surfaced and unsafe. Another motorist suggested unloading the top of the cargo, carrying it through the overpass, then reloading at the other side. During the discussion, a young lad eight or nine years old kept walking around the truck. Finally he attempted to get the truck driver's attention by tugging at his overalls. After several impatient brushoffs, the trucker demanded, "What do ya' want, Kid?"

"Sir," the boy answered, "why don't you let some air out of your tires and drive through? There's a service station on the other side of the bridge. You can fill 'em up again."

Jean Henri Fabre, the French naturalist, encountered processional caterpillars one day while he was walking in the woods. These unusual insects were marching in a long unbroken line front to back, front to back. *What fun it would be,* Fabre thought, *to make a complete ring with these worms and let them march in a circle.*

So, Fabre captured enough caterpillars to encircle the rim of a flowerpot. He linked them nose to posterior, nose to posterior, and started them walking in the closed circle. For days they turned like a perpetual merry-go-round. Although food was near at hand and accessible, the caterpillars starved to death on an interminable march to nowhere.

Doing business without advertising is like smiling at people in the dark. You know what you are doing, but no one else even suspects it.

A man ordered lobster in a luxurious restaurant. When the tuxedo-clad waiter brought the dish to the table, the customer looked at it and noticed that one claw was missing on his lobster.

"Why is he short a claw?" asked the customer.

The waiter looked down at the red creature, then hesitantly responded, "I don't know, Sir. Perhaps he was in a fight."

"Then take it back," the customer commanded. "Bring me the winner."

A group of primitive people who lived in a remote mountain village faced the perpetual threat of a water shortage. Each morning and night, every able-bodied person in the village carried clay vessels up the steep slope and filled them at the mountain lake. Every man, woman, and adolescent child spent two hours each day carrying water to the settlement. One day one of the citizens asked, "Why do we do this? There must be an easier way." He then climbed the mountain to the edge of the reservoir and with a crude tool—probably a stick, a stone, or a piece of iron—scratched a shallow trough leading to the edge of the village. Fresh, sparkling water followed him down the slope. At the edge of the village he trapped the precious liquid in a dish-like meadow. From that day on, two hours of time for every able-bodied person in the village was saved for more productive effort. In like manner, creative American minds have built physical plants to make life easier and more productive.

A student in a small Colorado college supported his family by pumping gasoline at a local service station. One day, in consultation with a psychology professor, the young man developed a customer-satisfaction study. For thirty days he recorded his sales without changing his usual work procedures. For another thirty days, he made two adjustments in his method. Whenever a line of cars formed at the pumps, instead of ignoring it, Marvin went to each motorist and said, "I'll help you in just a minute." To drivers already at the pump, instead of asking, "How many?" he said, "Shall I fill it for you?" At the end of the month, with his new approach, Marvin had incresed his gasoline sales by 150 percent.

Add Some Analogies to Your Set

Analogies are a special kind of illustration. They usually compare two unlike things that have one area of similarity. That area is powerfully persuasive or serves to clarify and create understanding. For example: If every dollar you earned were a pie and you were to cut that pie into pieces of various sizes representing your expenses, you would find that your food bill would be a large slice of that pie—*one-fifth of it.* Your housing bill would be nearly a fourth, and so on.

Analogies are very persuasive devices if the comparisons are closely drawn; that is, if the likenesses are apparent, acceptable, and logical to your listeners.

I'm going to include some sample analogies—just a few—as part of your starter set. Be alert for other analogies in your reading. Make up some of your own. It's great fun and excellent practice in creative thinking. As I present examples, I shall suggest how an analogy might be applied.

According to the Bible, as Lot and his family were leaving Sodom, they were instructed not to look back. Lot's wife, not heeding the admonition, looked over her shoulder and was transformed immediately into a pillar of salt.

Application: In business, if we live in the past, we cannot accept change. In sports, if we reflect on the mistakes of the last game, we shall repeat them in the game at hand. In life, if we rest on our laurels, we fail to work for the present.

Many golfers develop an involuntary habit that follows them through every round: As soon as the ball speeds away from the tee, they twist and contort their bodies as though to alter the flight. Their heads usually lean away from the line of flight in a vain effort to redirect the white sphere. Too late! Once the ball has departed it must run its course.

Application: Life's acts and decisions are very much like that ball. Once they have been made they must run their course. For the present, no amount of body english will alter the direction.

The boss may have reached the pinnacle of success, but he should never be without gratitude. Instead, he should think of a turtle resting in his shell on top of a post. That turtle did not reach this lofty height all by himself. Someone helped put him there.

Application: Success in life, in business, or on the playing field is usually a team effort.

Imagine you are bowling at an alley where the pins are covered so you can't see how many you knocked over after you throw the ball. Spectators are not allowed to cheer. The score of each line is put into a computer, but you never find out how well you have bowled until you receive the printout at the end of every quarter.

Application: Performance standards are related to immediate rewards and to rapid communication on how well you have done.

Some jobs are like lifting a bag of feathers. It isn't the weight that bothers; it's that you can't seem to get your arms around it.

Application: To accomplish a job, you sometimes need to break it up into smaller portions.

Suppose you have ten seeds to plant and that your livelihood depends on the *increase* you can get from those seeds. You won't throw them into any old plot and expect them to grow. You won't toss them down on a piece of clay and stomp them with your heel. On the contrary, you will select places where the seeds are likely to flourish, so that each will produce a harvest that will add constantly to your commodity storehouse.

Application: Every day has a finite number of hours. Within that number one can expect to spend a reasonable portion for productive effort. If livelihood depends on results—if a wasted hour is like a seed stomped into nonproductive clay—a person or a business that fails to control its time will never prosper in our competitive world.

A thermometer and a thermostat have something in common: They both are able to measure heat; however, a thermometer is a *passive* tool that measures heat and nothing more, while a thermostat is an *active* instrument—*it can command the temperature to change.*

Application: People have the option in their lives of being passive and reflective, or they can work to bring change to their environment.

Add Some Magic Quotations

The most accessible and readily available kind of support is quotations. The vast majority of older quotations are in the public domain. You are free to use them at any time because they are no longer protected by copyright.

If you choose quotations from contemporary remarks or printings, you should exercise caution, either giving credit or seeking permission to use the remark.

I'm going to include a few quotations for your starter set. Go on collecting your own. Quotations add power and credibility to your persuasive effort.

"A conqueror, like a cannon ball, must go on. If he rebounds his career is over."

—Duke of Wellington

"He who has the worst cause often makes the most noise."

—Old Proverb

"There is no security on this earth. Only opportunity."

—General Douglas MacArthur

"Institutions become great by the greatness of the men who champion them...by the greatness of the advocacy that defends them. A people indifferent to their civil liberties do not deserve to keep them. A people who proclaim their civil liberties but extend them only to preferred groups start down the path to totalitarianism."

—*Justice William O. Douglas*

"I am not always the same easy-going person. Neither is the weather always sunny and calm. Farmers know that both the sunshine and the rain, the cold of February and the heat of August contribute to man's welfare."

—*Jack Kaplan*

"Only when you have worked alone—when you have felt around you a black gulf of solitude more isolated than that which surrounds the dying man; and in hope and in despair have trusted to your own unshaken will— then only will you have achieved. Thus only can you gain the secret, isolated joy of the thinker who knows that a hundred years after he is dead and forgotten, men who never heard of him will be moving to the measure of his thoughts."

—*Justice Oliver Wendell Holmes*

"The time for learning anything is the time you need it."

—*Murray Lincoln*

"A boy has two jobs. One is just being a boy. The other is growing up to be a man."

—*Herbert Hoover*

"Let us endeavor so to live that when we come to die even the undertaker will be sorry."

—Mark Twain,
(from "Pudd'nhead Wilson's Calendar,"
in Following the Equator)

"America does not consist of groups. A man who thinks of himself as belonging to a particular national group in America has not yet become an American."

—Woodrow Wilson

"A wise man adapts himself to circumstances and environment as water shapes itself to the vessel that contains it."

—Chinese proverb

"Better to lose the anchor than the whole ship."

—Dutch proverb

"The most important ingredient of success is the ability to get along with people."

—Theodore Roosevelt

"The use of money is all the advantage there is in having money."

—Benjamin Franklin

"If you want to know if your brain is flabby feel your legs."

—Bruce Barton

"No man can be just a little crooked. There is no such thing as a no-man's-land between honesty and dishonesty."

—Herbert Hoover

"Only a mediocre person is always at his best."

—Somerset Maugham

"A thing is not necessarily true because a man dies for it."

—Oscar Wilde

"A long dispute means that both parties are wrong."

—Voltaire

"The greatest freedom that man has is the freedom to discipline himself."

—Bernard M. Baruch

"Keep your fears to yourself, but share your courage with others."

—Robert Louis Stevenson

"The way to stop financial 'joy-riding' is to arrest the chauffeur, not the automobile."

—Woodrow Wilson

"To speak without thinking is to shoot without taking aim."

—Proverb

"The body of man has the power to create whatever the mind of man can conceive."

—*Murray Lincoln*

"The question, 'Who ought to be hired?' is like asking, 'Who ought to be the tenor in the quartet?' Obviously, the man who can sing tenor."

—*Henry Ford*

"The proper study of mankind is man."

—*Alexander Pope*

"Mind is the great lever of all things; human thought is the process by which human ends are answered."

—*Daniel Webster*

"It is a shameful thing to be leery of inquiry when what we search for is excellence."

—*Cicero*

"Though the people support the government, the government should not support the people."

—*Grover Cleveland*

"Success or failure in business is caused more by the mental attitude even than by mental capacities."

—*Walter Dill Scott*

"There are two times in a man's life when he should not speculate: when he can't afford it and when he can."

—*Mark Twain,*
(*from "Pudd'nhead Wilson's Calendar,"*
in Following the Equator)

"The meanest, most contemptible kind of praise is that which first speaks well of a man, and then qualifies it with a 'but.'"

—*Henry Ward Beecher*

"The best of all governments is that which teaches us to govern ourselves."

—*Goethe*

"It is not strange that even our lives should change with our fortunes."

—*William Shakespeare*

"If you would create something, you must be something."

—*Goethe*

"Character is the result of two things: mental attitude and the way we spend our time."

—*Elbert Hubbard*

"Today is not yesterday. We ourselves change. How then, can our works and thoughts, if they are always to be the fittest, continue always the same. Change, indeed, is painful; yet, ever needful; and if memory have its force and worth, so also has hope."

—*Thomas Carlyle*

"When a man has not a good reason for doing a thing, he has one good reason for letting it alone."

—*Walter Scott*

"Let us not dream that reason can ever be popular. Passions, emotions, may be made popular, but reason remains ever the property of the few."

—*Goethe*

"Nature has given us two ears, two eyes, and but one tongue, to the end that we should hear and see more than we speak."

—*Socrates*

"The fortunate circumstances of our lives are generally found, at last, to be of our own producing."

—*Oliver Goldsmith*

"To most men, experience is like the stern lights of a ship, which illumine only the track it has passed."

—*Samuel Coleridge*

"Character cannot be counterfeited, nor can it be put on and cast off as if it were a garment to fit the whim of the moment. Day by day ... we *become* what we *do*. This is the supreme law and logic of life."

—*Madame Chiang Kai-shek*

"Mere obedience to the law does not measure the greatness of a nation. The true test is the extent to which individuals ... can be trusted to obey self-imposed laws."

—*Lord Moulton*

BUILD YOUR POWER WITH STRONG MATERIAL

The illustrations and quotations provided in your starter kit were selected at random. Many of them may not interest you because they do not support the kind of things you talk about. Don't make the mistake of discarding them, however, until you are sure you don't need them. Too much is better than too little.

Because only you know the kinds of subjects you talk about, only you are able to select the material that gives you the greatest power. In all your reading, in your conversations with others—even as you watch a movie on television—stories, analogies, and quotations pop out at you. Don't let them get away. Cast a net over them and transplant them at once into your speech file.

SUCCESS SECRET: An idea lost is an idea you may never find again.

A LOOK AHEAD

In the next chapter we shall continue to develop your speech file.

After a brief examination of humor—its characteristics and how to use it—I shall provide a starter set of funny and usable stories. You'll find them powerful as you prepare the introduction for your speeches and as you develop persuasive support for your speech points.

I hope you'll learn that humor is a magic tool for helping your audience to relax—to catch their mental breath—before moving on into heavier parts of your speech. Humor can be a stopping point that gives your listeners a brief rest between portages.

Let's go on to the next chapter and learn how to persuade with magic humor.

chapter 8

Persuade with Good Humor

A precious old story about inmates telling jokes in the penitentiary keeps popping up from time to time. In it the prisoners were allowed to spend two thirty-minute periods each day in the airing yard. Usually they sat with their backs to the wall and swapped funny stories. But the constricting time schedule severely limited the number of prisoners who could participate at each session. To correct the problem, one of the prisoners wrote all their stories in a book and assigned a number to each joke. Then the prisoners memorized every story and its corresponding number. Subsequently, whenever they were in the recreation yard, they no longer wasted time telling complete stories. Instead, whenever one of them called out a number, everyone laughed.

One day a new prisoner joined the group. On his first exposure to the airing yard, he was bewildered by the convulsive laughter that exploded every time an inmate barked out a number. His cellmate later explained to him what it was all about. Next day, anxious to try the system, the young prisoner sat beside his fellow inmates with his back to the wall. At the first opportunity, he shouted, "Sixty-eight!" Not a single laugh emerged from the group.

"What happened?" the newcomer later asked his cellmate. "When those other guys yelled out numbers, everybody laughed, but when I tried it they just sat there and stared at me."

"It's the difference in people," the cellmate explained. "Some can tell 'em and some can't."

145

His statement is absolutely true; *some can tell them and some can't.* There are people who by nature are not funny. They handle humor with neither skill nor confidence. I acknowledge too that there are successful, top-of-the-crop speakers who have no need for humor. In nearly every professional group—government dignitaries, educators, news media people, doctors, lawyers, and so forth—there are speakers who neither create nor try to create a ripple of laughter. These people are successful speakers because of who they are, what they know, or where they have been. Their popularity does not necessarily rest on their skill as persuasive spellbinders. Some may even have an intellectual bias against using funny stories. I know a speaker who thinks that humor demeans him. "If you want someone to be funny," he says, "let me know, and I'll bring a standup comic with me."

So be it.

> **SUCCESS SECRET: Most persuasive speakers can learn to use humor with beneficial results. Most audiences enjoy laughter. Funny stories bolster persuasion; they help to glue attention to the speech and to the speaker. Without listener attention, the speech is a waste of time.**

WHAT MAKES HUMOR FUNNY?

Psychologists have analyzed humor in an effort to discern *what is effective,* and *why it is effective*—in short, to determine why people laugh. Authorities agree that *the incongruous, the unusual,* or *the unexpected* (in the use of a word or in presenting the *punch line* of a story) stimulates laughter. For example, here is a story that contains all three of these elements. It is a tale that has grown old but never decrepit:

One Saturday night a farmer bought two sacks of groceries in the village store and carried them to his pickup. But he had failed to turn off his lights, so the truck's battery was dead. Unwilling to disturb his wife at home, the farmer thought to himself, *It's only a couple miles home. I'll just walk.*

To shorten the distance he cut through the cemetery, unaware that a fresh grave had been opened that afternoon. In the darkness the farmer stumbled into the open hole. Reacting with intense fright, he frantically explored the possibility of jumping out; then, after calming himself, he sat to ponder his plight. Realizing he couldn't reach the edge of the grave, he reassembled his groceries and settled into the corner to spend the night.

Shortly afterwards the village drunk left the local saloon and wandered into the cemetery. Meandering about, he too fell into the open grave. Screaming with fright, he jumped up and down clawing wildly at the walls of the hole. Suddenly out of the blackness came the farmer's baritone, "You might as well settle down. You aren't going to get out of here tonight."

BUT HE DID!

This is an excellent story to introduce a discussion on motivation. I have found it is versatile and it has a near-perfect audience response record.

And here is another illustration:

Two avid sportsmen, Henry and Jake, agreed to meet early the next morning and go fishing. At 4:30 A.M., Henry parked in Jake's driveway. So he wouldn't disturb others in the house, he went to Jake's bedroom window and tapped lightly on the pane. "Jake," he called. "Wake up!"

A sleepy voice filtered back through the glass. "What time is it?"

"Four thirty," Henry whispered.

"My gosh, Henry," Jake's sleepy voice complained. "You'd better go home and get some rest. We've got a big day ahead of us tomorrow."

How can you use a story like that? Half the fun of speech creation is fitting your story to the point you are making; or, to say it another way, to find the stories that perform a function for you. I once heard a speaker effectively use the Jake-and-Henry joke to close a banquet speech at the end of a long day in the convention hall. The audience loved him for his upbeat ending to a grueling day.

DELIVERY AND TIMING ADD MAGIC TO HUMOR

Using humor effectively can have a magic persuasive impact on your listeners. Success of humor depends upon the speaker's ability to tell stories or to pop a good one-liner. Work on the following factors for best results:

1. Select details that make the story clear and then add the embellishments that make it interesting. Leave out everything else.
2. Provide the proper vocal pitch and rate for creating mood and for transmitting the meaning of your joke.
3. Develop a graceful flair for pulling the trigger on your punch line.
4. Is your humor natural or is it strained? If your jokes are stiffly or artificially delivered, keep working to smooth them out. *Listen to a taped playback of your material. Skill comes from experience and from adaptation—and from confidence.*

Even the professionals have an occasional flop; so don't be discouraged if your humor now and then goes awry. Keep trying. Keep practicing. Keep learning. A funny story can create either a hilarious response or a dull thud. As you practice and as you learn to analyze the impact of your humor, you will notice that dull thuds become less and less frequent. You will create an inward sense for what will go and what will not. Furthermore, when you do reap a dull thud, your experience will teach you how to turn it to your advantage or to ignore it without destroying your self-confidence.

Listen to how other speakers do it. Analyze their techniques—how they use humor to enhance their persuasive power. Also try to study comedians on stage and screen. Certainly their objectives are different from yours for theirs is not a speaking situation; nevertheless, you can learn about timing, choice of detail, use of voice and all the other complex elements that wring laughter from a funny situation.

YOUR LISTENERS' MOOD MAKES A DIFFERENCE

Years ago when I was a college professor, a humorous incident developed in my classroom that destroyed the teaching environment for at least five minutes. That night at our dinner table, I recounted the happening. My family gave me a *laughter reaction score* of exactly zero. Brad, our youngest son, finally broke the distressing silence with a logical, forthright question, "What's funny about that?"

At that moment, I wasn't able to respond to Brad, but later the answer to his question was obvious. I should never have tried to transplant that incident to a place where the soil had not been prepared. In the classroom the original situation occurred naturally; there was psychological interplay among the students. As their professor, I too played a role. The students obviously had laughed in response to a mixture of related elements that could never be replicated in any other environment, particularly in an uncontrolled one—and specifically at my family dinner table.

One more example will emphasize the psychological side of humor:

> Many years ago, I delivered a speech with a good load of humor aboard. It was a roaring success (as measured by the laughter response). Two weeks later, I gave the same address with only slight modifications to a similar audience. From the beginning I sensed the *dull thud syndrome* permeating the room. Quickly, by substituting serious illustrations and quotations in place of the funny anecdotes, I was able to salvage the performance.

Although I made a good adjustment—and even a satisfactory speech—I was never sure I did the right thing. Perhaps the audience would have responded if I had persisted. I was uncomfortable and even afraid. My material was appropriate; I had tested it. The problem, however, may still have been mine for retreating prematurely when I realized I was on shaky ground.

> **SUCCESS SECRET: Study the many facets of your audience and of the occasion. Try to predetermine how well humor might be accepted.**

Evaluate Your Audience

Here are some things you should ask yourself as you prepare your speech, or as you contemplate whether to tell a complete story or drop a one-liner in the board room, at the dinner table, or in a social situation:

1. Do your listeners have some reason for not wanting to laugh? Although it is rare, some audiences, usually because of the occasion, do not want to laugh. A group of hostile stockholders may not be amenable to hearing funny jokes no matter how funny.

2. Have you taken time to set the mood for laughter? Speeches, right or wrong, often open with a "sure-fire

side-splitter." It is true that if the first story causes an eruption of laughter, the road ahead is usually open.

SUCCESS SECRET: No story is an island. It must fulfill a purpose within the framework of your speech or tie to the thread of conversation in an informal gathering. If used wisely and well, humor offers you its magic power.

People who use humor discreetly and professionally— whether on the public platform or in small groups— somehow seem to be more human and thus more likable. But those who misuse it can be awful bores. Don't destroy your personal magnetism by being a pest. Avoid dominating conversation with the jaded question, "Have you heard this one?" And remember, no one likes to be buttonholed at the watercooler by the office comic bubbling over with a new story he has just heard in the cafeteria.

Your power and appeal as a person are magically improved if you tell *only appropriate stories and only at proper times.*

Eleven Commandments for Using Humor

There are some rules you should observe, particularly *while you enjoy the privilege of commanding an audience from the public platform.* Discover how and when to be funny and you will also discover the radiation of magic power whenever you successfully generate laughter. Live by these rules; they will serve you well.

1. Don't hurt someone else's feelings or try to be funny at someone else's expense. Avoid stories about physical abnormalities. For example, anecdotes about stuttering may create real embarrassment. What about ethnic and religious stories? Although some speakers tell them successfully and tell them well, they generally should be avoided. At least choose and use them cautiously.

2. Avoid phraseology that brands you as an amateur. It goes something like this: "I understand it is appropriate to tell a story, so I found just the right one to introduce our speaker tonight." (Typically, the chairman then reads the story.)

3. Reuse your stories if they are good. If you discover a joke that always hits the mark, don't put it aside even if one or two of your listeners may have heard it before. A good story wears well, but don't go on with the stale and weary jokes. Remember, people cry, "Play it again!" for a tune they enjoy. For the familiar joke they groan, "I've heard it."

4. Test humor carefully if your audience is out-of-doors. Humor somehow evaporates in wide-open spaces.

5. Plan and select your humor more carefully for small groups of only ten to fifteen people. To obtain a laugh response from very small audiences is sometimes impossible. Spend extra time creating the mood for laughter. *Have a substitute plan available if your humor fails to take root.*

6. Don't telegraph the punch line. We've all heard the inept story-teller go on with a joke whose outcome the audience has already anticipated.

7. Don't step on your punch line. The fear that people won't laugh often prompts a speaker to move on too quickly, not leaving time for laughter to generate. Give it a chance to bubble.

8. Don't squirm if a joke or a one-liner should fail. Clever speakers can sometimes salvage it. Save it if you can, but don't make matters worse by trying to dredge up laughter that will not come. If the story makes a point, it really doesn't matter whether or not your listeners laugh.

9. Avoid impossible or ridiculous jokes. If they are totally unreal and unbelievable, leave them out of your speech until the time you can handle such stories with professional finesse.

10. Keep your humor close to home. Fit it to the community, to the audience, to the situation. For example, if you are talking to lawyers, use some lawyers as characters and some legal jargon in your stories. But don't overdo it. Giving all your stories a "lawyer slant" is a worse sin than not doing it at all.

11. Keep your stories simple and include only the relevant details. This does not mean that you cannot use long stories. I often do. Only be sure that the story is long because it has to be long, not because you have filled it with excess fat. Remember the old admonition: "If a *long story falls*, great is the fall thereof."

DON'T FRET ABOUT HUMOR STAGNATION

Nobody wants to listen to a string of worn-out, jaded, corny jokes, especially if they are read or poorly told. Obviously the way a joke is told and how it fits your material and the mood of your listeners all have a bearing on its effectiveness.

SUCCESS SECRET: A first class story, well told and properly placed, will nearly always elicit a laugh.

HOW TO CATALOG YOUR JOKES

In Chapter 7 you learned how to file your illustrations. I shall give you one more cataloging technique that is a variation—a refinement—on the prior methods. Evaluate this system. Compare it with the others; then use the one that works best for you. Perhaps the techniques from the last chapter might work well for your magic speech gems—your illustrations—and the one I present here, for your humor. You try them; you decide.

As in the methods I described earlier, this system also works with either a loose-leaf notebook or small white cards (three-by-five or four-by-six) for recording your stories. The filing procedure is essentially the same regardless of how and where you record the material.

Follow these simple steps:

1. Write the story on the card or on a page in your notebook.

2. Number the jokes in sequence as you acquire them. (Later in the chapter, I shall give you a starter set.) First, number the story on the left side of your card or in the margin to the left of the story in your notebook.

3. As you add a new joke, merely assign to it the next higher number.

4. After you have acquired a substantial number of stories, begin to classify them. You may need and use *200 or more classifying titles.* Common ones are

goal setting	economy	education
time management	honesty	motivation
creativity	aggressiveness	control
security	reward	leadership

Notice that the subjects *you* talk on will often determine the classifying words that you use. For example, people who speak on management subjects will obviously list delegation, time management, control, and the like. People who do philosophical speaking might lean toward words such as faith, honesty, brotherhood.

5. Set up a *separate card system* for your classifying index. Even if you record your jokes in a notebook, cards work better for the catalog because they can be shuffled and alphabetized. Three-by-five cards are the most desirable size. Use one card for each classifying word. Write or print that word in the top center portion of the card. Now write, in columns, the numbers of all of the jokes that fit

under that classification. If you add a new joke to your collection, obviously it will carry the highest number at that particular moment. Pull from your file the card that carries the classification of this new joke and add the number on that card.

I think it is obvious now how the system works. Example: If you need a joke on humility, find the card marked HUMILITY. On that card are the numbers of all the jokes in that category. By referring to the numbers in either your notebook or your card file, you immediately have the jokes you need. You will be pleased to notice that the numbers have automatically ascended in chronological order as you added to your collection. Every joke card in your file is numbered from one to the highest number in proper sequence. Every joke in your notebook is numbered in exactly the same way. Following is a sample of a classification card:

	PATRIOTISM	
1	35	54
21	43	65
27	46	74
32	51	82

How to use it. You need a joke on patriotism. You pull that card from your file box. The numbers on the card tell you at once which stories have potential for your purpose. Now go to your notebook or to your card box and find every card that matches a number on the card you have pulled. Immediately read each joke and determine whether or not you need it or can use it. If you are not sure, remove the card or the notebook page and put it with your speech preparation materials until you have made the decision. Sometimes, instead of removing the page or the card, I sketch the essential details of the joke on a work-sheet and put it with my other speech preparation materials. Each person must develop his own technique. Be sure, if you remove the card or the notebook page, that you restore it to the system after you are finished with it.

YOUR PERSONAL PACK OF MAGIC STORIES

A barber asked his customer, "Would you like a singe, Sir?"

"A singe? Why would I want one of those?" the customer inquired.

"To seal the tubes," the barber said. "When I cut your hair, I open up the ends so the oil runs out. That's why you're losing your hair."

The customer mulled this over for a moment and then said, "Look, since I was nineteen years old, I've been shaving every morning. I always cut off my whiskers, but my beard never falls out. How would you account for that?"

The barber responded quickly. "I would account for that by saying that you aren't the kind of guy that story was made up to be told to."

A businessman reported to his staff: "This project report somehow gives me the same feeling I had last week when my six-year-old asked if syrup is good for the carpet."

A man encountered a friend he had not seen for a long time. "Say," he said, "I heard your brother made $50,000 in a cattle deal in Wyoming last year."

"Well, that's essentially true, except it wasn't my brother, it was my brother-in-law. And it wasn't Wyoming, it was Montana. And it wasn't last year, it was two years ago. Not cattle, but sheep. And he didn't make it, he lost it."

Three umpires were discussing their officiating techniques on the playing field. One declared, "Some is balls and some is strikes, and I call 'em like I see 'em."

The second umpire said, "Some are balls and some are strikes, but I call 'em what they are."

The third bragged, "Some is balls and some is strikes, but they ain't nothin' 'til I call 'em."

A group of employees bought their supervisor a get-well card while he was hospitalized. At the bottom of the card they wrote, "The office gang send their best wishes for a speedy recovery—by a vote of seven to four."

A guest speaker waited through a long, tedious program for his turn on the platform. Half a dozen others preceded him, and as each finished his remarks, more and more of the audience departed. Finally when it was the guest's turn to appear, only one person remained in the auditorium.

The speaker said, "Sir, I want to thank you for staying around to hear me speak."

"Don't thank me, Fella," the man answered. "I'm the next speaker."

A banker and a farmer were out on a lake fishing in a small rowboat. Suddenly the farmer stood up, tipping the boat and dumping both of them into the lake. As the farmer attempted to salvage their gear, he realized that the banker, who couldn't swim, was bobbing up and down in the water. "Can you float alone?" he called out.

The banker sputtered, "Here I am drowning and you want to borrow money."

A lady entering a bakery shop discovered a seven-year-old alone behind the counter. "Where are your parents?" the customer inquired.

"Across the street having coffee," the youngster replied.

"Aren't they afraid you'll eat all of these nice things?"

"Nope," the child answered. "They made me promise I wouldn't—but I lick some of them."

The man declared that he never played golf because it made him sad. "Every time I see someone who plays as badly as I do," he said, "I start feeling sorry for him."

A very poor but loving family lived in the hills of Tennessee. One night, by skimping, the mother was able to serve twelve hamburger patties to her husband and their brood of nine children. On the first serving each took one hamburger, but all of them longed for the remaining one on the platter. Suddenly a blast of wind blew out the candle. The mother rose to relight it. When she returned to the table, her husband's hand had nine forks sticking in it.

A bottle washed up on the shore of an island where three men had been stranded for many months. One of the men pulled the cork from the bottle, and a genie flowed out. As is usual with genies, it promised to grant one wish to each of the captives. Two, who were family men, wished they could go home and were promptly whisked away. The third said to the genie, "I'm not homesick, but I'm very lonely. I wish my friends were back."

Near the end of a golf round in which Mr. Jones had played his usual bad game, he said to his caddy, "I'm sorry about my inept golfing. I'm sure it makes your job difficult."

The caddy replied, "Mr. Jones, think nothing of it. I've enjoyed caddying for you. I've been working this course for nineteen years and today I've been in places I've never seen before."

A man moved into a metropolitan area but would not travel about because he was afraid of the freeway traffic. One day he confessed his fear to a neighbor who suggested that he drive on the freeway during a low traffic period until he established his confidence. "What is the best time?" the newcomer asked.

The neighbor replied, "I'd recommend Sunday morning. The Roman Catholics are in church, the Protestants are in bed, and the Jewish folks are all up at their lake places."

So, on Sunday morning the man drove timidly onto the superhighway and immediately collided with a Seventh-Day Adventist.

An old man boarded an airplane in Columbus, Ohio, for his first plane trip. Before takeoff he watched the handlers loading baggage and saw the Marriott truck storing food aboard the plane. At Detroit he stayed on the aircraft and watched the activity on the tarmac. Finally the plane reached Minneapolis. While waiting for the service doors to open at the gate, a passenger next to the old man looked at her watch and said, "Say, we made good time."

"I should say," the old gentleman answered, "and that Marriott truck really travels fast, too."

A speaker once asked his audience if anyone had ever met a perfect man. No one had. He then asked if anyone had ever met a perfect woman. One woman raised her hand. "You have met a perfect woman?" the speaker asked her directly.

"Well, no, I've never met her," the woman answered. "But I've heard a lot about her. She was my husband's first wife."

When the nineteenth-century theologian Phillips Brooks, was on his deathbed, many of his ministerial friends attempted to visit him, but were always turned away. One day, the famous agnostic Robert Ingersoll went to the hospital to see Brooks and was admitted at once.

"Why is it," Ingersoll asked, "that you permitted me to come in, but you turned away all of your Christian friends?"

"I'll have plenty of chance to see them up above," Mr. Brooks said, "but this may be my last chance to ever see you again."

Someone has come up with a solution to the conflict between college football and academic responsibility: have one team for offense, one for defense, and one to attend classes.

Former governor, Earl Warren of California, was taking a ribbing from former Illinois governor, Adlai Stevenson, because of California's consistently bad showing in the Rose Bowl games against Big Ten teams. "Boast on," Warren said, "but remember this: a whale never gets harpooned until it comes up to spout."

Quick thinking: When Pastor Jacobson saw Mrs. Erlich (whom he detested) coming up the front walk, he retreated to his study upstairs. Later he shouted to his wife, "Has that awful bore left yet?"

Rising quickly to cover the embarrassing blunder, his wife responded, "Yes, Dear. Mrs. Erlich is here now."

Two golfers had just finished putting when a golf ball rolled onto the green. "Let's make that guy think he got a hole in one," one of the men suggested. He moved the ball into the cup. Almost at once the owner appeared on the green. "You guys see a ball come up here?" he asked.

"Yes," one of the other golfers responded. "Man, what a shot. Your ball's in the cup."

"Oh good," the golfer exclaimed. "That makes only seven on this hole."

A camper in New Mexico killed a rattlesnake one night after supper. Later he decided that the rattles would make a good souvenir. In the dark he arose and cut the rattles off the tail. The next morning as he came out of his tent, the color quickly drained from the camper's face. The snake he had killed still had its rattles.

"Don't ever look back," a supervisor cautioned his staff in a training session. "Once you've committed yourself to a goal, never look over your shoulder. Remember Lot's wife in the Bible? She looked back at Sodom and turned into a pillar of salt."

"That's right," an enthusiastic young trainee confirmed. "The same thing happened to us. My wife was driving the kids to school, and when she looked back she turned into a telephone pole."

Tony and Mark worked together in the warehouse. Every noon they sat on the dock and ate their lunches. Tony would invariably open his lunchbox, remove a sandwich, and examine it to see what kind it was. If it was peanut butter, he threw it away. Any other kind he always ate. One day Mark asked, "Tony, how long have you been married?"

"Twelve years," Tony said.

"You've been married twelve years, and your wife still doesn't know you don't like peanut butter?"

Tony retorted defensively, "You leave my wife out of this. I make these sandwiches myself."

Two young boys, loose and alone in a department store, were licking ice-cream cones as they rode up the escalator. One lad noticed that his cone was dripping, so he wiped it on the fur stole on the lady ahead of him. "Watch out, Tommy," his friend cautioned. "You're getting hair all over your ice cream."

After waiting a week, a woman confided to her husband that her credit cards had been stolen. The husband decided not to report it to the police because the thief was spending less than his wife had been spending before the robbery.

A woman asked her husband, "Who's this Ethel person you talk about in your sleep?"

"She's not a person," her husband explained. "It's a horse the guys at the office bet on."

That evening, as the husband came in from work, his wife announced, "Your horse called you today."

It is a citizen's duty to support the government, but not necessarily in the style to which it has become accustomed.

A large company offered a prize of fifty dollars to the employee who submitted the best idea for saving money.

The winning suggestion: "Reduce the prize to twenty-five dollars."

A grumpy husband came to the breakfast table displaying his usual domineering attitude.

"What'll you have for breakfast?" his wife asked.

"Two eggs. Fry one. Poach one," he demanded.

A few minutes later his wife placed the breakfast in front of him. He glanced at the plate then snarled at her, "Take it away. You poached the wrong one."

One night a highway patrolman stopped a car along the road to inform the driver that his taillights weren't working. The driver walked to the back of his car and immediately began to cry.

"Look," the patrolman said sympathetically, "it's not all that serious. I won't give you a ticket for just a taillight problem."

"Who cares about a ticket?" the motorist shouted. "Where's my boat?"

A poorly prepared program chairman introduced the banquet speaker. "I don't know much about our speaker," he said, "but I'm told he's very good. If that's true, we'd better get on with it. If it isn't true, we'd better get it over with."

Americans are people with strange priorities. They set aside one day a year in tribute to mothers and reserve a whole week to recognize pickles.

A woman camouflaging her age is a good deal like an automobile: a fresh paint job conceals the blemishes, but the lines usually give away the model.

A top executive died and was dispatched to Hell. As soon as he arrived, he began in typical fashion to give orders. He commanded one group to carry out ashes, another to stoke the furnace, and a third to engage in an energy-conservation study. Within a week, the devil summoned the executive to his main office. "Look," the devil said, "I've been watching you. I don't know who you think you are, but you act as if you own this place."

"I do," the executive declared. "My board of directors gave it to me before I came down."

People can learn much from the tenacity of elephants. An executive hurrying home for his wife's dinner party was delayed at an intersection by a circus parade. He rolled down his car window and asked a policeman, "How much longer will it be?"

"Not very long," the policeman assured him. "The elephants are next, and they're the end of the parade." The driver sat watching eighteen elephants linked together, trunk to tail, as they passed by. Then he gunned his engine and spurted into the intersection. Too late, he saw a baby elephant at the very end of the line, her stubby trunk firmly latched to her mother's tail. A few days later, the executive's insurance agent telephoned to say that the circus had submitted a claim for $165,000.

"A hundred sixty-five thousand dollars for one baby elephant!" the executive exclaimed.

"It wasn't just the baby," the agent explained to him. "You pulled the tail out of eighteen other elephants."

A young bride was cooking a ham for their first Sunday dinner. She cut it in two pieces before she put it in the oven.

"Why'd you do that?" the admiring husband asked.

"Gosh, I don't know," she replied. "My mom always cut the ham in two, but I never asked her why."

The next day the young woman telephoned her mother to inquire about the procedure. "I don't know either," the mother explained. "Your grandmother taught me to cut the ham in two. Next time we see her we'll have to ask."

A few weeks later, the grandmother came for a visit. At the first opportunity, the young bride asked the older lady why she had always cut the ham in two before she put it in the oven.

"Oh heavens!" the grandmother exclaimed. "I'd almost forgotten about that. When I was first married my pan wasn't big enough for a whole ham."

Two older men were reminiscing on the front porch one night. "Remember, Henry," one of them said, "how we used to go out and paint this town red?"

"Sure do," Henry replied. "But I reckon if we'd do that now it'd be three or four weeks before we'd be strong enough to give 'er a second coat."

As a college professor opened his front door to leave for work, he discovered that a steady drizzle was falling. Automatically he reached for an umbrella only to discover that the umbrella stand was empty. One at a time the professor had carried them all to the university and left them there. A young lady sat next to him on the bus and chatted pleasantly as they rode along. When they reached the university stop, the professor absent-mindedly picked up her umbrella and turned to go down the aisle.

"Hey," the lady complained, "I believe you have my umbrella."

"Oh dear, I'm sorry," the professor apologized, embarrassed over his unconscious act.

That night as he prepared to return home, he picked up all the umbrellas in his office and carried them onto the bus. Coincidentally, the same young lady was already aboard. "Say," she called out brightly. "You really had a good day."

After his first jump, a parachutist was visiting with a friend. "What did you feel," the friend asked, "just before you jumped out of that airplane?"

"I felt two things," the parachutist replied, "panic and a real hard shove."

The doctor counseled a business executive after having given him a thorough physical examination. "You absolutely must get more exercise," the doctor said. "Why don't you begin walking to work?"

"Why, I'd be bored to death," the patient complained.

"You don't need to be," the doctor argued. "Make a game of it. Buy a hoop and roll it to work with a stick."

The businessman took the doctor's advice and soon found himself enjoying the trip as he rolled his hoop to and from work every day. He even made arrangements to store the hoop in a parking garage near his office.

One night when the executive went to the garage for his hoop, the attendant told him that a car had accidentally run over it. The businessman became very distraught.

"Don't worry, Sir," the attendant assured him. "We'll buy you a new one tomorrow."

"Tomorrow! That's a big help. How am I going to get home tonight?"

In response to a newspaper advertisement, a young lady applied for a job. "You are really wasting your time," the personnel director told her. "I've received over fifteen hundred applications through the mail."

"Well," said the applicant. "Why don't you hire me to screen them for you?"

A naked man wearing a barrel for protection walked down Seventeenth Street in Denver. A patrol car pulled up at the curb and intercepted him. "Are you a poker player?" the policeman asked.

"No," the man replied, "but I just left some people who are."

A young lady wrote home from college: "Dear Mom and Dad, I am sorry I haven't written for awhile, but since the dormitory fire, when I jumped out of the window and broke my leg, I haven't felt well. Fortunately it didn't hurt the baby. As soon as Jim's divorce is final, he's going to marry me, and I just know I'll love both of his kids."

"Ha-ha," her letter continued, "I fooled you! There was no dormitory fire and no broken leg. And there's no baby or a marriage to a divorced man. But I am getting an 'F' in English and I want you to put it in proper perspective."

The farmer announced he was writing out instructions for his funeral. "I'll ask the banker to be one of my pallbearers," he said. "He's carried me this far, so he might as well take me the rest of the way."

A door-to-door salesman approached a house where a huge black dog guarded the front step. "Will your dog bite?" the salesman inquired of a youngster playing in the front yard.

"Nope," the child answered.

The salesman advanced towards the house only to receive a vicious nip on the leg. "I thought you said your dog doesn't bite," he snarled at the little boy.

"He don't," the boy replied indifferently. "That ain't my dog."

A family was being uprooted by a company transfer. Four-year-old Joey, who had never moved before, was unable to comprehend the commotion and excitement. On the night before their departure, Joey closed his bedroom prayer with, "Goodbye, God. Tomorrow we're gonna' move to Iowa."

When a person is eager to do something new, he boasts, "You are never too old to learn." However, if he doesn't want to do something, he says, "You can't teach an old dog new tricks."

A speaker said, "I'm like the guy describing Kentucky as the state of beautiful women, fast horses, warm bourbon, and productive blue grass. I do hope that I got all those adjectives in the right place."

Perhaps someday we will hear that medical science has created a new miracle drug that works perfectly on human beings, but it won't be available to white mice for three or four years.

Several youngsters were overheard discussing their arrival into the world. Little Timmy was confident that the doctor had brought him. Janie seemed sure that her parents had bought her at the department store, but Johnny thought he had been delivered by a stork. After much thought another youngster in the group said, "My folks were awfully poor. I'm sure I was homemade."

Charlie's wife nagged him constantly for spending long hours at the office. One evening on his way home, Charlie passed a factory where mules were used to pull heavy equipment. Just as the five o'clock whistle blew the long-eared beasts dashed pell-mell to the gate, fighting and pushing each other to get out. Charlie thought to himself, *I must let my wife see this so she'll know what a clock watcher looks like trying to get away from the job.*

The next evening Charlie went home early, picked up his wife, and timed his driving to arrive at the factory precisely at five o'clock. When the whistle blew, he pointed to the jumping and fighting mules as they fought their way to the entrance. Charlie said, "Look at that. What conclusion can you draw from those animals?" Without pausing, his wife replied, "Even a jackass knows when it's time to quit."

On the days that Jerry drove in the carpool, he always stopped beside the state insane asylum and watched one of the inmates pitching all by himself in a make-believe game of baseball. One day, one of the riders asked Jerry, "Why do you stop and watch that guy winding up and pitching every morning?"

"Well," Jerry explained, "the way things are going at the office, it won't be long before I'll be in there catching for that guy, and I want to study his curve."

In the Biblical days, Moses and the tribes of Israel approached the Red Sea with the Egyptians in hot pursuit. Moses was in a quandary. Behind him lay death; ahead of him lay an insurmountable barrier. He summoned his engineers and said, "Let's build boats and get these people over the water." The engineers shook their heads and said, "There is neither enough material nor time to build vessels."

"Then let's build a bridge over the water," Moses suggested. "Surely you can put up a temporary structure that will carry us across." The engineers still shook their heads and said, "That cannot be done."

"Summon my public relations man!" Moses shouted. "He's a man of ideas. He'll solve our problem." The public relations man listened to the problem, then asked for a little time to think about it. He entered his tent and stayed for many hours while Moses paced impatiently up and down the beach. Finally as the sun began to drop into the western skies, the public relations man came out of his tent and looked across the water. "Have you found an answer?" Moses asked. The public relations man shook his head and said, "I'm sorry, Sir. I agree with the engineers. There is no way." Moses was furious with him. "All my people are incompetent," he shouted. "I'll solve the problem myself. I'll separate the waters and march my people through on the floor of the sea."

The public relations man stared at him with surprise and said, "Sir, you do that, and I'll get you two pages in the Old Testament."

A car stopped along the road to pick up a hippie-type hitchhiker. When the long-haired young man got into the car, the driver noticed that he was wearing only one shoe. "Did you lose a shoe?" he asked.

"Nope," the hitchhiker replied. "I found one."

"Times do change," the salesman said. "I remember years ago when I left home my wife always said, 'Clay, you watch out for all those blonds and brunettes and redheads.' Now she says, 'Be careful of what you eat.'"

The bookkeeper burst into the manager's office to inform him that their company was out of the red for the first time in five years. "Wonderful!" exclaimed the proud businessman. "Make up two dozen copies of our financial statement and mail them to the bank and all my creditors."

"I can't do that," the bookkeeper declared. "We'd be back in the red again."

Why do they call it rush-hour traffic when it's always standing still?

The pilot on a coast-to-coast plane leveled the craft at 33,000 feet. Unaware that the switch to the cabin intercom system had accidentally been turned on, he said, "Man, I could sure use some coffee and a little lovin' from the new cabin attendant."

The hostess, dashing up the aisle to caution the pilot about his oversight, was intercepted by a little old lady sitting in the aisle seat. "Honey," the passenger said, "you forgot the coffee."

Grandpa bought a new hearing aid that was absolutely undetectable. After wearing it for a couple of weeks, he called the salesman to express his satisfaction.

"I'll bet your family likes it, too," the young salesman said.

"Oh, they don't know I got it," Grandpa chuckled. "And am I ever having fun. In the last two weeks I've changed my will three times."

A little boy came to the dinner table with a dark purple ring around his eye. His father asked very casually, "Who gave you the black eye?"

"They don't give you black eyes," the boy retorted. "You've gotta' earn them."

An elderly lady collapsed on the sidewalk. Immediately another lady knelt to administer aid, and a crowd of curious onlookers formed a tight circle around them.

"Back up," someone called. "Give her air."

"Give her some whiskey," a man shouted from the ring.

"Loosen her clothing," still another suggested.

"Give her whiskey," the man repeated.

"Get her some water," another stranger shouted.

The old lady who had collapsed suddenly sat up on the street. In a shrill voice she shouted, "Why don't the rest of you shut up and listen to that guy that wants to give me whiskey."

Two boys were involved in a classic argument. "My dad can lick yours," one boy declared.

"Big deal," the other answered, "so can my mom."

A boy came home from school with a very poor report card. He decided that a good offense was his best defense. Handing the card to his father he said, "Dad, I got three 'Fs' on my report card. Do you suppose my problem is heredity, or environment?"

Control is the ability to idle your engine when you feel like stripping your gears.

The store manager sent in a big order for merchandise. He received a telegram back: "Can't send shipment until you pay for the last order."

The retailer immediately sent back a collect telegram: "Can't wait that long. Please cancel the order."

The company's system was very slow to respond. Someone described it as being like a reptile wrapped around the world. Step on the snake's tail, and two days elapse before it yells, 'Ouch!'"

From time to time everyone has made excuses for being late, but a high school student who lived on a small acreage gave his principal the most unusual explanation for tardiness. He said, "I'm late because my dad sleeps in his underwear."

The principal, pressing the young man for further explanation, received a full account.

"A fox has been stealing our chickens," the boy explained, "so last night, my dad put the double-barreled shotgun behind the kitchen door before he went to bed. During the night he heard a commotion in the yard, so he went out and pointed his gun at the chicken-house door. About that time, our collie-dog came up behind and touched my dad's leg with his cold nose. That's why I'm late; I've been picking chickens since four o'clock this morning."

A building superintendent reported to his employer, a real estate developer, that a house had collapsed when the scaffolding was removed. "I've told you a dozen times," the developer scolded, "never take away the scaffolding until the wallpaper is up."

A man who hadn't kissed his wife for five years promptly shot the man who did.

Two salesmen attended a friend's funeral. After the service one of the salesmen said, "Old George sure didn't look very good. What did he have?"

The other replied, "I think it was North Dakota."

A young man reported to the airport for his first parachute jump. The pilot noticed that the lad appeared to be afraid. "Don't worry about it," the flier said. "When I slow down the airplane, just jump out and count to five. Pull the rip cord, and it will open up above you. Then you'll float down to the ground, and there'll be a truck waiting to pick you up. If the chute doesn't open, reach over and pull the auxiliary cord. On the ground the truck will be there to pick you up."

At three thousand feet, the neophyte jumped. He counted to five and waited for the chute to flow out above him. Nothing happened, so he pulled the other cord.

Still no pressure from above. "By golly," he muttered, "the way my luck is going I bet that truck won't be waiting for me either."

After an angry dispute with his supervisor, a man quit his job and walked out the door. Soon another worker went in to the supervisor and said, "I'd like to apply for Willie's vacancy."

The supervisor replied, "I'm sorry, but Willie didn't leave a vacancy."

During the Depression, two commuters were sitting next to each other on a streetcar. One of them who was reading the paper said, "My, my, but this Depression is terrible."

The other answered, "Yes, and isn't it too bad that it came along when so many people are out of work."

A woman who was filling out a credit application was asked how much insurance coverage her husband had. She didn't seem to understand the question, so the interviewer phrased it differently, "If your husband should die, what would you get?"

The lady thought for a moment and then answered, "I think I'd get a parakeet."

"I don't think I'm going to have any more arguments with my son about borrowing the car," a man confided to his friend.

"How's that?" the friend asked.

"From now on, whenever I want it I'm going to take it."

The barn on Farmer Smith's farm burned to the ground. In due time, Mr. Smith received a letter from his insurance company that read, "We have carefully examined your claim and have arranged to send out a crew and build you a new barn."

The irate farmer, who had anticipated receiving cash, wrote back an angry letter: "If that's the way you pay your claims, you can just cancel the insurance on my wife."

Taking advice from him is like taking navigation lessons from the captain of the Titanic.

A machine worker named Butterworth was afraid of his supervisor. Butterworth trembled whenever the boss approached his lathe. One day Butterworth came to work with a high fever. The man at the next lathe, noticing Butterworth's discomfort, said, "Say, you're sick. Why don't you go home?"

"I don't dare," Butterworth answered. "The supervisor would fire me."

"He'll never find out," the neighbor declared. "He took the day off."

With this assurance, Butterworth removed his shop coat, went to his car, and drove home. As he climbed the front steps he glanced in the window, and there was the boss kissing his wife. Horrified, Butterworth hurried back to the shop and returned to his lathe.

"I thought you went home," the man next to him said.

With a scornful look, Butterworth said, "Fellow, you almost got me in trouble!"

DON'T WEAKEN YOUR PERSUASIVE POWER

Speakers who have a vast repertoire of stories are sometimes misguided in using them. There is a strong temptation to tell a story merely for the sake of the story. Sometimes a speaker does this without having any real purpose in mind for doing it. There are speakers who can virtually stop the flow of their talk and tell stories. Usually they create this hiatus between points, but sometimes they pop them right into the middle of a point and then return to the mainstream of their speech, very cleverly accomplishing the feat.

While I was in the middle of writing this chapter, I took time out to make a speech in Milwaukee. The chairman that night was an experienced platform person, a man who has done much training in the field of management. I led him into a discussion of using humor as I have described it above. His response was very practical: "Never forget that humor is often a mood. If the speaker has created a very serious mental fix in his listeners and suddenly breaks it with a funny story, how can he possibly reestablish his credibility no matter how funny the story might have been."

This man went on to point out that two dangers are imminent.

1. The mood of the speech itself is destroyed.
2. The story itself will bomb because it is incompatible with what the listeners are doing mentally at that moment.

I consider this a very sound analysis from an experienced speaker. As a general rule, a great amount of skill and experience are prerequisites for this kind of humor. One might even say that there are few instances where that rule ought to be broken.

The more tightly a speaker organizes, the less likely he is to display a disjointed presentation that destroys rather than enhances his power. Before you try it be sure you know what you are doing, that is, be natural, comfortable, and graceful. Be sure you do not destroy your magic power by seeming inept and disorganized.

In a similar way—though I am repeating—I admonish you again to *be sure your humor fits.* I restate my earlier counsel: Don't drag your funny jokes in by the heels.

Example and Application

A friend of mine visited a tractor-assembly plant in China. He learned that the tractor parts were being made in widely scattered locations and then brought to this plant for final construction. He also learned that the Chinese, under this scheme, were having tolerance problems on some of their parts. My friend inquired, "If a part is too small, how do you assemble it?"

The supervisor confided, "We hammer a lot."

Many speakers connect their jokes and illustrations in the same way. They reach far out to bring them into the outline. *They hammer a lot.*

GO ON COLLECTING

In Chapter 7, I encouraged you to keep adding to your collection of magic illustrations. Do the same thing with your file of good humor. Be alert for funny stories. Remember that few of them are ever new. For some reason, humor often reincarnates itself and reappears after an absence of many years. If a joke performs well, fit it in and go on using it. You'll know when it no longer meets the test of time.

Skill Builders

I have combined the Skill Builders for Chapters 7 and 8. The techniques and the exercises are identical for both chapters.

1. Return to Chapter 7 and select an illustration from your starter set of stories. Read it—truly concentrating on its details. Read it again, but *do not memorize it verbatim.* When you feel you have mastered the essential details, stand in front of a mirror and tell the story, capturing its mood—sadness, excitement, suspense, and the like. Be natural. Be relaxed. Be sincere. Let the *meaning* of the illustration flow out so you can virtually feel the hush that comes over your imaginary audience.

2. Next, select and carefully word the premise that is supported by this illustration. Stand in front of the mirror. State your premise; *then deliver your persuasive illustration,* tying it together with a clear transitionary statement.

3. Now let's rearrange your approach: Practice giving the illustration first, then applying it to the premise. *Deliver it with power and conviction.*

4. This time add another illustration as well as a quotation to support your premise. Continue to practice various arrangements similar to the following:

    I. Premise
      A. Illustration
      B. Quotation
   II. Reiterate Premise
      A. Illustration
  III. Restate Premise

Remember—your objective is to gain acceptance for your premise. Keep practicing until you feel magic power in your presentation.

5. Return to Chapter 8 and *repeat all of the above steps,* this time using humorous illustrations.

6. To practice humor for opening your speech, return to Chapter 1. Briefly review the techniques for breaking the audience barrier. Now, *create and practice a two- or three-minute speech opening using jokes from your starter set of humorous stories.*

PRESS THE MAGIC-MEMORY STAMP

Humor is an essential part of the speech. Let it play a magic role.

Observe, listen, practice, so you can be one of those "who can tell 'em," and tell them well.

Humor is not a symbol of intellectual inadequacy. Be discreet. Be moderate, but don't avoid a funny story.

Humor relies on the incongruous, the unusual, and the unexpected, or a combination of these elements. Identify which element is contained in your story. It will help you deliver the story effectively.

Choice of details and feeling the movement or rhythm of the story will help you to present it well.

Don't unleash a joke unless the mood of your listeners is right. If the audience is intensely serious, only the most clever speaker can make it work and will probably realize he shouldn't even try.

I gave you *eleven commandments* for the magic power of humor. Go back and read them now. Return and read them often.

Keep adding to your collection of magic stories. The power of a superior persuader is stronger when the well is deep and forever filled.

Establish a usable system for cataloging your jokes, but don't let the task become onerous; don't let it frustrate you. I've found it is better to thumb through the stories often—to become familiar with many or all of them—than to expend valuable time trying to be a catalog perfectionist.

A LOOK AHEAD

The spontaneous speech—the kind you give on the spur of the moment—is difficult. Presenting it can be a fear-filled experience *until you learn how to do it properly.*

Because interviews, conversations, and small group participation are usually *spur-of-the-moment* situations, they too can be frightening *until you learn to handle them.*

In Chapter 9 you will discover how to cope with these impromptu occasions. An infallible formula for quickly constructing your presentation or response will provide the confidence you need. You will learn to make a good impression on your listeners, even though you are expected to speak without any advance preparation.

chapter 9

Use Personal Persuasion for All Occasions

As your speaking reputation grows, you will receive many invitations to perform on the public platform and in small meetings. You will introduce other speakers, answer questions in front of a group, interview and converse—even be called on for spur-of-the-moment or impromptu speeches.

Although these activities may not seem like major speaking engagements, you should never treat them with indifference, approach them without preparation, or perform them in a haphazard manner.

> Never botch the introduction of a speaker. *Learn how to do it well.*
>
> Don't feel inadequate in a question/answer session. *Learn how to do it well.*
>
> Don't disintegrate when asked to speak without prior notice. *Learn how to do it well.*
>
> Develop your own conversation skills.
>
> Don't be afraid of one-on-one encounters.

All speaking occasions are important—some to the success of a meeting, always to you as you expand your persuasive power.

SUCCESS SECRET: Good speakers perform well in all acts of persuasion.

Obviously, your reputation for consistency is uppermost, but so is your obligation to the people you serve as a

183

speaker. Look on every occasion as a challenge to do your best, for example, an opportunity to "merchandise" another speaker as you introduce him, or a chance to draw people out as you converse with them or interview them.

A good guideline—a starting point—in preparing for special situations is to determine the bare essentials that need to be spoken. A friend once suggested that I use *one question as a touchstone* in preparation: "What really needs to be said?" This admonition is particularly beneficial in conversation and in certain special speaking assignments. Be brief. Be miserly with your words. I don't imply that your sentences should be short and choppy, but I do mean that you should carefully choose the essentials—the very best material available—and express only the relevant facts.

Although time at special functions and in conversation is usually limited, never set out to be merely a time-filler; *never just pad.* Choose essential material, organize it well, say it persuasively, and then stop. By following this rule you will display your power and demonstrate your mastery of persuasion.

HOW TO HANDLE THE SPONTANEOUS SPEECH

Your Skill Builders have laid a strong base for facing the spontaneous or impromptu speech. You have developed the power to do it well. Now you merely need to transfer that power to the event itself and do it with confidence.

Warning: Fear is often the strongest enemy of the impromptu speaker.

Suppose you are participating in a meeting where a controversial resolution is being considered. The motion is on the floor to request that the highway speed limit be increased by ten miles an hour. You are opposed and wish to express your opinion. *You have a spontaneous speech coming on.*

Or, you are a personnel director participating in an executive staff conference. The corporation vice president addresses you: "Charles, what growth do you predict in personnel requirements for the next six months?" *You are about to make a spontaneous speech.*

There are several steps you should take. After a bit of practice, the system becomes nearly automatic.

1. Think of yourself as an authority. Let a feeling of competence flow through your system. This performs wonders for your confidence level.

2. Ask yourself, *What needs to be said?* There is no time for irrelevant material. Plan to take tight aim for a rifle shot at the subject.

3. Allow yourself as much time as you can gracefully acquire for thought and organization. Don't begin to talk until your brain is ready.

4. Use the "premise/support" technique for your persuasion. It is a superior method for bringing maximum power to the spontaneous situation.

How to Use the System

Begin the speech with your premise—with the point you are making—then add your reasons and your "for instances." Let's return to that speed limit resolution. You believe the speed limit should be fifty-five miles an hour. State your premise with a strong, persuasive declaration: *"Our safety and our welfare are guarded by a fifty-five mile-an-hour speed."* That is your *premise*—the peg on which you will now hang your material. Unless you were aware beforehand that this subject would be debated, you probably do not have specific facts on hand, particularly statistics and quotations. Because you have strong feelings on the subject, however, you do have general support material in your mind.

For example, here is a sample skeleton of what you might say.

1. *State your persuasive premise.*
2. Our automobile death rate declined at once when the reduced speed limit was imposed and enforced nationally.
3. Recently, a friend of mine had a serious accident. Investigating officers agreed that death might have resulted if either car involved had been traveling above fifty-five miles an hour.
4. Petroleum is in short supply. High-speed driving causes engines to gulp fuel.
5. *Restate your premise.*

Obviously, the more specific you make your support and the more concrete you make your illustrations, the more persuasive your speech will be.

In the second instance, as a personnel director, you might state: *Personnel requirements ought to increase by 3 percent in the next six months.* You might support this positive premise with specific examples that include the following statistics:

1. The Information Systems Division plans a growth of one percent to accommodate the increased demand for product information.
2. The vice president of marketing told me yesterday that he will need 4 percent more people by August.
3. Most companies like ours are anticipating a 3- to 4-percent employment growth. For example, Ajax Consolidated Foods has built in a 3-percent expansion to adjust for significant increases in product movement.
4. *It is reasonable to predict that our company ought to plan a 3-percent increase in personnel during the next six months.*

Sometimes in highly controversial matters an abrupt statement of your premise raises defenses and makes persuasion more difficult. The signals are sent out during discussions, occasionally electrifying the air. In some contentious matters the dispute may have raged over a long period of time, and people may have become seriously polarized. Withhold statement of your premise to the end.

I once attended a meeting in which school consolidation was being proposed. Parents—particularly rural people—harbored strong resentment toward a plan to transport their children by buses to areas outside the home communities. One of the advocates of reorganization played a powerful, persuasive role at the meeting by making two spontaneous speechs, both organized under the *premise/support* type outline. *But she withheld the premise statement because of the extreme antagonism toward school reorganization.* She first presented her support material, thus making the premise more palatable when she finally presented it at the end. None of the opposition had disappeared, but it had been reduced, and the audience began to lean on this woman for advice because of her common-sense persuasion. Here are the two conclusions she capably presented in her spontaneous speeches:

1. Our children will be safe traveling to school on well-supervised buses.
2. A superior education for our children is impossible in small, inefficient school units.

USE THE SPONTANEOUS SPEECH TO ANSWER QUESTIONS

The *premise/support* system is ideal in a question-and-answer program. It is lamentable and unnecessary that even mature, well-informed people dread the pressure of answering questions. Once, at a corporate annual meeting where I spoke, the president confided to me that after thirty-two years of facing the stockholders he had never lost his fear of answering their questions.

Thirteen Rules

Let's look at some methods that would help him, and you, develop magic power in this fear-ridden exercise.

1. Remember that *you are the authority* or you wouldn't be answering questions in the first place.

2. To answer a question, ask yourself, "What needs to be said?" *Keep the main premise* in mind. Thoroughly answer the question, but don't say more than you need to.

3. Don't be afraid to say, "I don't know." This is a lesson that most beginning school teachers have to learn. What's the sin in admitting you do not have the answer? Take a raincheck. Answer the question at tomorrow's session, or if the session is adjourning, mail the answer to the inquirer's home.

4. Don't be evasive. If the question should not be answered for any reason at all, say so. Avoid the overused, "No comment."

5. Ask the question to be repeated if you haven't heard it or if you don't understand it. Use the technique also to buy time. It is remarkable how quickly your brain will generate information during that brief interval when the question is being restated.

6. State your premise. Add your support and call for the next question. Too frequently, speakers spend a quarter-hour or more answering only one question. Only the most complex inquiries require more than a two- or three-minute answer.

7. Repeat the question for the audience if necessary, so that everyone will quickly see how *your premise and the*

question are neatly related. This adds immeasurably to your prestige and power.

8. Avoid an ongoing dialogue with only one member of the audience. Always involve and address the entire audience. If other listeners cannot hear, or if they feel left out of the action, you will quickly lose control.

9. Don't forget your eye contact and body language. They are as important in a question/answer session as in a main address.

10. Discreet use of humor will relieve tension—yours and the listener's. If the audience seems to react adversely, drop the levity at once. I once heard an irate listener shout at a speaker, "Look, we didn't come to hear your wit."

11. Keep your cool. Never get angry. It is defensive behavior. It disrupts your poise. *Remember, shouting is not personal persuasion.*

12. Terminate the question-and-answer period by announcing you will answer a specific number of additional questions—one, two, three; you decide.

13. To provide persuasive impact and a professional finish, cap the session with a strong thirty-second, motivating summary.

WHEN YOU HAVE TIME TO THINK

Occasionally you have time to "prepare" the spontaneous speech. You may have a hunch you will be called on for an opinion (a conclusion). For example, you may be in a business meeting waiting your turn to take the floor. In those few moments you cast your ideas. I like to use the "thought-tree" method as a trigger. In the trunk of the tree I write the main idea (my conclusion which often flows out of the separator funnel. See Chapter 7). Each branch becomes a suggested support item from which I select the ones I shall use in my speech. Usually I conjure far more than I need. The system helps me to visualize the "spontaneous" speech I am about to make.

Here is an incidental suggestion: I keep a packet of blank thought trees in my brief case. They help me to discover the components of the many topics and problems I need to analyze.

HOW TO INTRODUCE A SPEAKER

Speakers need a good introduction; yet many chairpersons either make the task laborious or do a shoddy job—or both.

Preparation for the introduction should begin well in advance of the performance. Learn all you can about the speaker, his background, and his topic. Ask yourself: *Why was this speaker chosen for this audience and for this occasion?* The answer to that question will provide substantial material for the introduction itself.

Be sure you know how to pronounce the speaker's name. If you can visit with the speaker prior to the meeting, do it. Ask if there is something special he'd like to have you say when you introduce him. Find out if there is something special you should avoid saying. Perhaps you can make a statement that will be an excellent springboard for a good launching.

How to Organize a Persuasive Introduction

The chairman tells a short, funny story, reads a long biographical account of the speaker, and then says, "I'm proud and pleased to present our speaker, Major Hiram Anderson." Such is the phrasing for a typical introduction—a very poor introduction. Most speakers deplore it because it is boring, embarrassing, and ineffective.

A speech of introduction should be as persuasive as any other kind of speech. It should be animated and exciting. As a probable beginning point, there has to be a

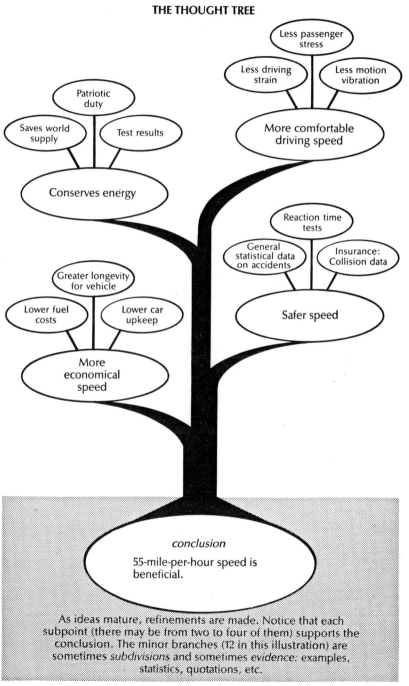

THE THOUGHT TREE

Less passenger stress

Less driving strain

Less motion vibration

More comfortable driving speed

Patriotic duty

Saves world supply

Test results

Conserves energy

Reaction time tests

General statistical data on accidents

Insurance: Collision data

Safer speed

Greater longevity for vehicle

Lower fuel costs

Lower car upkeep

More economical speed

conclusion
55-mile-per-hour speed is beneficial.

As ideas mature, refinements are made. Notice that each subpoint (there may be from two to four of them) supports the conclusion. The minor branches (12 in this illustration) are sometimes *subdivisions* and sometimes *evidence:* examples, statistics, quotations, etc.

Art by Roger Jensen

reason why this man or woman was invited to speak at your meeting.

> Do you have a problem the speaker can help you solve?
>
> Can he or she motivate your members to greater achievement?
>
> Is the speaker—as an officer of your association, your church, or your corporation—about to deliver an important annual message?
>
> Has this speaker been invited to present special educational information to the audience?

Whatever the reason, use it directly or indirectly as you make the introduction. Add an interesting illustration or quotation that suggests the mission of the speaker. (It may be a funny story if humor is appropriate). For example, suppose the speaker is an expert on business forecasting. You might begin like this:

> A great man once said, "He who can foretell events will win success in all he does." If all of us could only possess that power, think of the gains we might make in our business ventures or in our personal investments.

All of this alludes to the problem—and to the opportunities—that this speaker will probably talk about. At this point therefore, notice how natural it is to focus at once on the speaker himself. Let's go on:

> We'd like to have power to predict the future. With his peculiar background and his complex bank of computers, our speaker has learned how to do it. He knows how to make remarkably accurate forecasts of economic and political events—and has made them for some of America's leading corporations.

Now, work in the salient facts about the speaker's background. Keep it general. Pick out the unusual, the exciting things he has done. (Who cares where he went to high school?) Don't make the speech. Don't even try to guess what the speaker plans to say. Keep the introduction short.

You are now ready for a climactic, persuasive ending. *It's so simple:*

> Would you like to know how to tell what lies ahead? Maybe (*Insert the speaker's full name*) will tell us how we can do it. Let's welcome him and listen to "How You Can Foretell the Future."

In brief the following is a reliable outline for any speaker introduction:

1. Begin with an interesting quotation or illustration that alludes to the state of events in the speaker's topic area. (Hurry to your speech file. It's your best friend.)

2. Select fascinating facts about the speaker. What qualifies him or her for the presentation? Promise a reward to the audience.

3. Summon the speaker to the lectern.

SUCCESS SECRET: Introducing a speaker should be an exciting and comfortable experience for everyone.

Use Persuasive Power When You Present a Speaker

Here are some reliable suggestions.

1. Don't try to steal the show. Many chairpersons unconsciously upstage the speaker during the introduction or after the speech. The speaker is the expert. It is his or her day. Don't usurp it.

2. If you use humor be sure it is appropriate *and plausible.* Don't tell a story simply because some people feel it is the traditional thing to do when a speaker is introduced. If the speaker is a stranger to you and to the audience, it might be advisable to omit all jokes, although an atmosphere sometimes develops at a meeting that

opens the door for storytelling. If so, it is a natural and appropriate thing to do.

3. Don't give the speaker's speech or present your views on the subject either at the beginning or the end of the speech.

4. Some introductions have lasted as long as twenty minutes. Don't let it happen to you. Make it interesting and keep it brief.

5. When you present the speaker, invite, and even lead the applause.

MASTER THE ART OF PERSONAL CONVERSATION

Have you ever noticed how easy it is to visit with some people but that an invisible barrier sometimes seems to exist between you and others?

Some interviews follow the same pattern. Perhaps you are screening applicants for a job or soliciting information for a magazine article. From the opening contact some persons immediately release lively conversation. Time flies like sand emptying from a timer glass. But some applicants, in response to your questions, open and close like oyster shells. Each comment is a sum of two or three words.

Analysts tell us that the difference is in the "chemistry" of people. Some individuals blend and some don't. If this theory is true, then it is preordained that some people will never be able to engage in relaxed, enjoyable conversation.

Nothing can be farther from the truth. The secret lies in being a *conversational catalyst,* an agent that brings people together and draws them out. *Here is a chance for you to use your magic power of personal persuasion.*

Good persuaders are usually good conversationalists because they know where and how to direct their attention. They possess a learned ability to converse without strain. In their presence there is nearly always a natural exchange of lively, worthwhile dialogue that is compatible with the occasion. *You are that kind of person.* So is my friend Arlene.

I call on Arlene whenever I need a competent catalyst in any group. For example, once I had to entertain four young French students at lunch. All of them were able to converse in English. I asked Arlene to join us. For only a few moments after we sat down to eat was there any lull in the conversation. I sat back, relaxed, and listened to the galloping conversation. Within a few minutes our French guests, with eyes shining, were standing in a linguistic queue waiting to ask questions and to participate. At an opportune point, I directed the talk toward the subject that was the reason for our coming together, and by the end of our session the mission had been accomplished.

What is Arlene's secret? How is she able to acquire the same satisfactory results with nearly everyone? You'll discover that next.

How to Make the Magic Catalyst Work

For most people, relaxation in conversation is more difficult than any other kind of personal contact; yet, there is no speaking situation where relaxation is more important. *Tension and relaxation are both progressive in their influence;* that is, they generate themselves—in opposite directions, of course. If you are relaxed, others will relax with you, and both of you will tend *to hold that relaxation* unconsciously until something occurs that causes tension. Then, unless bridled, that tension will grow progressively. Because of our psychological makeup, it is unfortunate that tension sprouts more readily than relaxation. The tension of one partner in dialogue or one person in a small group can contaminate everyone else in the circle.

A comparison between tennis and badminton makes the principle more understandable: In tennis you drive hard—hit balls (*tension*) back and forth across the net. Tension over, tension back. In badminton, a relaxed "bird" flies idly over the net, flutters against the other player's racquet, and then floats back to you.

A good conversation should not be a strenuous effort. If tension dominates, you frequently end up saying silly things or sending artificial signals that don't depict the real you at all. If you are struggling for responses you automatically create inward stress and begin to "play tennis."

> **SUCCESS SECRET: Be yourself. If people think of you as phony, whatever you are doing to impress is probably phony.**

I have a friend I've known for more than twenty years. In group activities we've had hundreds of good times together, but if caught alone as two people, our conversation quickly dries up. A trip together in a car seems interminable. Scores of times I've tried to draw him out. I still work at it, and he has probably done the same to me. Both of us have failed. I don't know why. I only know that our time together is compounded silence.

In contrast, I once chanced on a man in a coffee shop at the state capitol in Pierre, South Dakota. We entered an easy, spontaneous conversation. The next day I encountered him again. Later we became close friends. Never was there an uncomfortable silence between us. Even when words were not flowing, silence itself seemed to utter thoughts.

The secret of personal persuasion in small groups lies in six major areas.

Six Rules to Help You

1. Do all you can to give relaxation a head start. Do not approach the occasion with negative thoughts about your performance. Remember: Both tension and relaxation are progressive.

2. Discover common ground in conversation as quickly as possible. If it is found at once, tension cannot take root.

3. Direct your attention outward. Avoid indulging in self-occupation. Too often we are concerned about what others see in us, and usually it is a negative fear:

My clothes are wrinkled.

I'm not expressing myself well.

She doesn't like me.

These are fearful tension builders that afflict a large number of people. Avoid them. Think instead that *all these things are right*—or don't think of them at all. Don't be concerned about someone else's appraisal of you. You are probably wrong anyway. Let the arrow of your attention point the other way. Look at your partner or at the listeners in the group and ask yourself instead

What do they like?

What do they do?

What have their experiences been?

Soon, you will discover that this new frame of mind has a positive affect on you—and you begin to "play badminton."

4. Listen with genuine interest. Instinctively we seem to want to talk about ourselves. We wait for the slightest pause in conversation and jump in with a monologue as though we were afraid of encroaching silence. Avoid the irrelevant tale and there might be no silence, for failure to listen slows up and deflects the quest for common ground. Look at the speaker. Absorb what's being said. Let body language play its part. Soon you will detect a distinct improvement in your personal power. Success is the inevitable result, and success from one experience helps you avoid tension in future conversations.

> **SUCCESS SECRET: Persuasive power in conversation depends on personal magnetism, not high-pressure dominance.**

> **SUCCESS SECRET: Listen with interest. Don't drive your ideas like wedges into a split log.**

5. *Save up response ideas.* Often a bit of forethought yields all kinds of things to talk about, all sorts of topics you can explore with your conversation partner. Toss out response ideas instead of delivering detail-filled monologues. *But do it with apparent animation instead of planned intent.*

> **SUCCESS SECRET: Response ideas are good props if you prevent them from becoming artificial.**

6. *Don't panic over moments of silence.* It is not the fearful thing it sometimes appears to be. Often—most of the time—communication is occurring even when words are not being spoken.

Silence does have two dangers, though, that should be avoided:

> Don't let silence become a moment when your mind returns to its old habit of negative self-appraisal.

> Fight off tension. Conversation will soon return if you don't block the channel with encroaching stress. Ten seconds is not an eternity.

LET'S PRACTICE

Skill Builders

1. To practice selecting important details for spontaneous persuasion, imagine that your baggage has been

lost by an airline. Write down only the essential data the airline needs for locating your property and returning it to you. You may have a tendency to overcommunicate. *What really needs to be said?*

2. Select the name of a well-known person, one about whom biographical data are readily available. Pretend you are a member of an association that has invited this person to speak at its meeting. Write down the answer to these questions:

Why was this individual invited?

What special persuasive function do you expect this speaker to perform?

What are this person's qualifications for the assignment?

Using your answers, create an introduction for the speaker and practice delivering it. Use all of the powers of persuasion that you have acquired.

3. Make believe you are facing a group to answer questions about a subject on which you are well-informed. Write down some typical questions that might be asked. Six or seven should do. Record the questions on tape *as if you were actually receiving them from the audience.* Leave a few seconds of blank tape between each one. Make them sound real. Now stand before a mirror and persuasively answer each question as it plays out of the recorder. Repeat the question if you need to "buy time." State your conclusion. Present your examples and other support. Keep your answers brief.

4. Imagine you are conversing with someone with whom you are often ill at ease. "Think in" the usual silences, and relax your way through them. Toss out response ideas. Repeat this mental exercise several times, then physically confront this individual. *You will enjoy the improvement.* Continue practicing this conditioning skill until it works consistently for you. You will discern a general improvement in your personal persuasion that will carry over into all of your conversation and small-group contacts.

PRESS THE MAGIC-MEMORY STAMP

The special persuasion functions are as important to the occasion as a full-length speech or presentation.

Always ask yourself, "What needs to be said?"

The spontaneous speech should be compact. State your premise persuasively. Support it with powerful examples, quotations, and statistics.

If there is dissension over a plan or a proposal use your support *first* to break ground and soften the opposition. Then state your premise.

Keep your poise and confidence. They are keys to magic power.

Practice using the "thought tree." It helps you to dredge up ideas.

To introduce a speaker well, always learn all you can about him. Tie in this information to the occasion and to the needs of the audience. Be animated in your presentation. Never neglect the magic tools of persuasion. Help the speaker do a good job by giving him a powerful launching. Be brief.

Happy interpersonal relations are a characteristic of successful persuaders. Be a catalyst that induces a relaxed, harmonious blend among people. Direct attention away from yourself. Listen attentively. Don't forget to toss out response ideas.

A LOOK AHEAD

The world of science has created some sophisticated tools that add great power potential to our speeches and presentations.

Projection equipment, when needed, can persuade with visual illustration. And, of course, we still have available the old standbys: the chalkboard, the chart board, and the flannel board.

With good amplification you can control your voice, yet project it into the farthest corners of the auditorium.

These tools are a persuader's assets, but they can detract unless we use them efficiently. In the next chapter you will learn to use the magic power of visual and audio support. Let's turn to this last branch of personal persuasion.

chapter 10

Harness Visual Aids for Persuasive Power

There is an old Chinese saying, "I hear and I forget. I see and I remember." Although concrete examples are a form of *seeing* (because they create mental images), there are times when *visual support* adds strength to your persuasion. It is generally conceded that we recall only 10 percent of what we hear, but 65 percent of what we both *hear* and *see*. These numbers are significant enough to make us consider visual support for some of our persuasion projects.

KINDS OF VISUAL SUPPORTS YOU CAN USE

The chalkboard is a time-honored visual device, especially effective in small groups. Its flexibility makes the chalkboard a popular tool for seminars, board meetings, and other small groups. Chart boards, although smaller than chalkboards, provide a major advantage: They can be professionally prepared in advance of the meeting. For example, I present an annual seminar on group dynamics for a group in the Middle West. After two years of trial runs, I engaged an artist to prepare my charts. I store and transport them in a four-inch mailing tube. The meeting host provides a mounting easel.

As with the chalkboard, you can also write on blank sheets of chart-board paper, drawing your visual illustrations with felt-tipped marking pens as you go along. Using different colors adds interest to the page. If you have a flair for sketching and lettering you can do some magic things on the paper.

Overhead transparencies have become a popular and easy way to illustrate speeches. Projectors are available nearly everywhere. The overhead projection film can also be professionally prepared in advance. It is easy to transport in a file folder or a large envelope. Inexpensive color processes have enhanced the attractiveness and increased the effectiveness of transparency support. Overlaying separate sheets of film to build composite illustrations also enhances interest and increases persuasive power. Some speakers develop illustrations as they speak by drawing directly onto the film with special colored pens. If type and images are made large enough, transparencies can be used with groups of several hundred people.

Probably the most frequently employed kind of visual support is the use of 35-millimeter slides. Some speakers carry their own projectors, but usually this is unnecessary; the equipment is available almost everywhere.

The slide system is very flexible because slides can be arranged and rearranged quickly and easily in the tray. By projecting them on a large screen, hundreds of persons can see the visual images without difficulty.

Some sophisticated slide shows, programmed through computers and shown on giant screens, are sometimes presented by convention speakers. They are expensive productions. Executive speakers from large corporations frequently use them. Because the system is not readily available to most of us, there is little need to discuss it further.

Flannel boards, at one time a very common visual system, are not as popular with modern speakers, but they do have merit. They can challenge your creative energy and provide good visual support for small-group presentations. Once it is constructed, a flannel-board program becomes somewhat permanent in format, but it usually retains its impact. Static electricity holds cutout figures, words, and other visual items onto the flannel board. The elements can be easily shifted about and arranged in any pattern. Folding boards are available that open into a wide expanse, thus providing a larger visual surface, yet keeping the flannel board small enough for easy portability. As the speaker proceeds through his presentation, he adds elements to the board. Used properly, the system can be an exciting and powerful auxiliary to your speech.

TEN METHODS FOR VISUAL PERSUASION

Remember, you are striving to persuade other people. To attain this you must follow specific guidelines for using visual support.

Here are some suggestions to help you.

1. *Use an expert artist to prepare your transparencies and chart board sheets.* Persuasion and professionalism are companions. Speakers dilute the power of visual support by transferring typewritten material direct to the film. Frequently the type is faded. Always it is too small.

2. *Don't overload the medium.* A slide, transparency, or chart with too many elements is cluttered and distracting. Nothing pops out at the listeners.

> **SUCCESS SECRET: Don't print your entire speech on a visual medium. Select details that give supplementary force to your personal persuasion.**

> **SUCCESS SECRET: Don't commit "image overload," then try to read your way out of the morass of facts and figures.**

3. *Adjust the size of the visual images to the expected number of listeners and viewers.* For a presentation in a large auditorium, make larger images, or obtain a larger screen and move the projector farther back than you would in a small room before a limited audience.

4. *Rehearse to ensure a smooth presentation.* Fumbling with a visual, dropping it out of sequence, or displaying uncertainty does not increase persuasive power. It is more likely to destroy your strength.

5. *Construct meaningful images and sentences if you create them while you talk.* I once heard a speaker say, "Don't pay attention to what I write on the chalkboard. I use it so I'll have something to do with my hands." When he finished, the chalkboard was a swirl of meaningless abstractions. The speaker would have been more persuasive without a chalkboard, for he used it only as a crutch for his own nervousness.

6. *Your spoken words should not merely repeat what is on the screen or board.* Let the slides illustrate your points. Let your words amplify the screen's message.

7. *Keep the visuals simple and uncluttered.* Be sure the basic message of the visual is clear at first glance.

8. *Avoid identifying statements about a slide.* Do not say, "This is a fertilizer plant." Instead, try this: "The miracle of abundant harvest begins in a phosphate plant." If a picture of the plant is on the screen at that moment, everyone knows what it is, and you are performing like a professional persuader.

9. *Use visuals only when they provide the greatest power.* As a rule of thumb, if you are using slides, plan to change every ten to twelve seconds. Don't continue projection of a slide for more than fifteen seconds.

10. *A lively voice must accompany visuals in a darkened room.* A moribund tone will soon put your listeners to sleep.

FOUR WAYS TO ENSURE GOOD PROJECTION

Following are some physical considerations that can add to or diminish your persuasive power:

1. Be sure that light levels in the room are proper for projections. Experiment before the program begins. Arrange in advance for someone to dim the lights. Be sure that your helper knows where the switches and dimmers are and how they function.
2. Mount 35-millimeter slides into plastic frames. Cardboard mounts sometimes stick in the projector.
3. Provide adequate lighting for the chalkboard, flannel board, or chart board. Avoid glare and reflection.
4. Do not block the view of your audience by standing in front of your visuals.

Cuing transparencies and 35-millimeter slides creates the special problem of making changes at the proper moment. One of the most reliable methods—the only one if you are speaking without notes—is to make the changes yourself as you speak. Advancing slides is accomplished with a remote control unit that you hold in your hand or lay on the lectern. You energize it by pressing a button to bring up a new slide.

Transparency changes are more tricky because you must lift the film from the projection deck and replace it with another. With a bit of practice, most speakers learn to make changes gracefully; however, if you cannot do this with ease, it may become a source of distraction, and the activity may interrupt your train of thought.

Having someone else change your transparencies is a good alternative, especially if you are reading from a script. Provide the projectionist with a marked script. Placing a conspicuous dot wherever a change is desired is the simplest and best method.

Another option is awkward and generally diminishes the power of your presentation. It is the verbal request method—an oral command, "Next slide please." *I recommend this system only as a last resort.*

Once I worked closely with a speaker who invariably used visuals. She spoke without notes, but discovered that changing her own slides always ended in chaos. Although she couldn't remember to use the remote changer, for some reason she could press the switch on a tiny penlight that she concealed in the palm of her hand. Whenever the light flickered, the projectionist received his cue. The method always worked, and it permitted this speaker to perform with maximum power.

HANDLE THE MICROPHONE PROPERLY

Microphones are commonplace in our electronic society, but it is amazing how many people fear them—and generally don't know how to use them properly.

Microphones never bite. They are real friends in time of acoustical need. Only now and then will one be an enemy, and that's usually caused by faulty public-address equipment. I once spoke to a medical group in a luxurious hotel in the Black Hills of South Dakota. The group was transported by bus from Rapid City, and we did not arrive in time for me to inspect the amplification equipment. It was a hopeless piece of antiquated junk. My voice sounded as though it were being filtered through several layers of bubbling water. I look back on that experience as one of my most *unpersuasive appearances.*

Only a responsible meeting planner insisting on satisfactory equipment can avoid calamities like this. As a speaker, try to protect yourself by making inquiries about the amplification system long before the date of the meeting.

Microphone Mountings

Microphones are usually mounted on a floor stand or on the lectern; or they are attached around the neck as a lavalier. Often by requesting a specific kind it will be provided for you. Many microphones can be removed from the floor stand and used as a hand-held mike.

I prefer the lavalier with a long cord so I can move about. As mentioned earlier, I often carry a cordless microphone, a system with a tiny transmitter that goes into my shirt pocket. It has a separate receiver that feeds the auditorium amplifier. In spite of occasional incompatibility problems, the cordless mike is an ideal tool that permits me freedom to use my arms for persuasive communication and to move about without tripping over cords.

Six Tips for Using the Microphone

1. Try to obtain a "level check" with a competent technician before the meeting begins. Determine the most effective distance between your mouth and the microphone. At the same time become familiar with the sensitivity pattern in front of the instrument—180 degrees, 90 degrees, and so forth.

2. Learn how to raise and lower the microphone stand if it should be necessary. People do come in different sizes.

3. If you need to determine whether or not the microphone is open (turned on), *do not blow into it.* The moisture and the blast can injure the mechanism. Besides, the sound is annoying. Instead, tap lightly on the sensitive side of the microphone or say, "Test."

4. If you increase your volume during any portion of your speech, back off ever so slightly. The tiniest movement, in or out of the range, makes a substantial difference in the sound level. Watch your listeners. Their expressions will telegraph their annoyances and your audibility.

5. Decide whether or not you want to hold the microphone. If you decide to keep it in your hand, practice using it. Even experienced speakers occasionally forget to maintain proper distances between the mouth and the mike. Remember: Too close—distortion. Too far away—"Can't hear you!" The hand-held microphone gives you mobility—it lets you leave the lectern and amble about.

6. Be careful not to create extraneous noises that are readily amplified: moving your hand on the shank of the hand-held microphone, the lavalier-mike brushing against a tie or neck scarf, drumming with your fingers on the lectern deck, or turning the pages of a script.

Four Alternatives if the Amplifier Fails

Be a coolheaded professional even if amplifier problems occur. Don't panic. Consider your options.

1. Discard the system and go on.
2. Wait for someone to repair it.
3. Ask if there is a standby system.
4. Don't ask questions like, "Is this thing on?" An expert knows whether or not he's getting through.

LET'S PRACTICE

Skill Builders

1. Make a rough sketch of a billboard in your community including all of the elements it contains: photographs, attention copy, address or telephone number, and the like. Where did your eyes first fix themselves on the billboard? Where, and in what direction did they move next? Using the same layout principles, develop a visual illustration for the topic, "*How* not *to use a microphone.*"

2. Again, using the billboard principle you have discovered, sketch a visual for one minor point from one of your own speeches. (Don't bother about artistic excellence.) Test it with the following questions:

Does the idea come through at first glance?

Is it simple? Uncluttered?

Keep practicing. Notice how your visuals become more powerful as soon as you have learned two or three basic principles.

3. Find a place where you can experiment with a live microphone. Your church might do, or a school auditorium, or perhaps the conference/training room at the corporate office where you work. If you can, take someone with you as a test listener. Practice handling the mike. Move in and out of its sensitivity pattern; move closer, then farther away. Study the effect on the amplification qualities. Speak louder, then softer. As often as you can, experiment like this. You'll soon discover your magic power smoothly flowing through a public address system.

PRESS THE MAGIC-MEMORY STAMP

Visuals can make your material more memorable; hence, your persuasion becomes more permanent.

Chalkboards, chart boards, flannel boards, slides, and transparencies are the main kinds of visual media.

Visuals should be neat, simple, and uncluttered. Their meaning should be clear at a glance.

Practice working with your visuals so you don't drop them or fumble with the sequence.

Make the size of your visuals proportionate to the size of your audience.

Establish proper light levels in the meeting room both for your projected visuals and for spotlighting your boards.

Locate the light control equipment before the meeting begins.

Never block your listener's view of the visuals. Practice protecting their sightlines.

Pick in advance the best method for changing slides and transparencies.

Be at peace with your microphone. Learn its characteristics. Remember you may usually select a mounted, a hand-held, or a lavalier-type mike.

Avoid bad habits at the microphone: blowing into it, coughing into it, drumming on the lectern, or moving in and out of the sensitivity pattern.

A LOOK AHEAD

Your magic power has beome well-rooted. With each speaking appearance and experience, your personal persuasion has grown stronger—more powerful.

Now, you are ready for a pep talk and for pressing the final magic-memory stamp.

Move into the finale and read how to *compound the strength of your persuasive power.*

chapter 11

How to Compound Your Persuasive Power

You have come a long way since Chapter 1. You have learned to persuade by properly using both body and voice. You have developed confidence in front of an audience, in a group discussion and in a conversation with a companion across the table.

When you began reading this book and first set out to do the exercises, you probably were *not* a neophyte speaker, but now you have attained an even higher level of proficiency. You have become a *master persuader*. To compound your power, keep the words *communication* and *persuasion* ever in the forefront of your attention. Remember this: *Always aim at your listeners*. Communication requires it, and without communication there can be no persuasion.

Investors who are skillful in handling their money like to receive compound interest. Each day their earnings increase because the principal grows progressively larger. In much the same way your persuasive skills expand with every new experience. You add finesse and confidence. You become sensitive to listener signals. You organize material for persuasive results. Consciously or otherwise you are compounding your skills for greater personal power. New knowledge added to the old is like interest in the bank, making you a richer, more competent persuader. There are several ways to compound your persuasive strength. Let's look at them.

BE MENTALLY AND PHYSICALLY PREPARED

How you feel in the period of time *before* the speech, the meeting, or the conversation has an important influence on how well you perform.

My speaking colleague, Chris Christianson, whom I have frequently referred to, often gives a talk entitled, "You Can't Lead a Cavalry Charge if You Don't Think You Look Good on a Horse." And you can't be a persuasive speaker if you don't feel comfortable at the lectern. In the old days of radio there was a comedian who played the role of a door-to-door salesman. Each time he approached a house, he said over and over to himself, "I hope nobody's home, I hope, I hope." This is a classic example of *defeat before encounter.*

Self-deprecation and improperly administered self-criticism breed incompetence and stem the flow of creative improvement. If that silent voice deep inside keeps repeating and repeating, "They'll laugh at you," or "You won't remember what to say," then indeed you are on a collision path with failure. Let yourself believe you are incompetent, that you are awkward, that you have nothing worthwhile to say, and sure enough these things tend to come true. Never, never submerge yourself in negative thoughts. "My clothes don't fit;" "That man in the front row is sneering at me;" "People won't listen to me;" or (the dreadful fear that used to engulf me) "What if people get up and walk out?"

> **SUCCESS SECRET: Thinking success won't necessarily transport you to the pinnacle, but believing you will fail practically drops failure at your doorstep.**

To compound your persuasive power:

Tell yourself you feel good—you feel good physically and feel good about yourself. Bubble with enthusiasm over your message and your opportunity to express it. How many

*others have the same chance? It is you and you alone
appearing on this platform. All of those people out there came
to hear you. What a wonderful privilege.*

Make the most of it. No one wants you to fail. Believe
that. It's true. They came to profit from what you have to
say and you should enjoy the privilege of presenting it.

Athletes frequently talk about the need for team effort
and the psychology of winning. I like to think of public
speaking, or any other spoken presentation, as a team
project. Members of the team are

1. The speech itself, carefully prepared.
2. One's mind, sharp and ready to perform.
3. The body, well-groomed and relaxed.
4. The listeners—receptive, relaxed, and supportive.

Every speaking occasion is a chance to marshal the
forces of the team. Focus on what you are saying NOW.
Prepare for it. Plan your strategy—the game plan—then,
like the athlete, *believe in yourself.* We've all seen the
baseball player approach home plate with the bat resting
comfortably on his shoulder, a determined expression
etched on his jaw. He stares at the pitcher. Although no
words are spoken, the message is clear and certain. "Go
ahead and throw, Mister. That ball is going for a long, long
ride." He knows it, and you know it, *and it goes.* You can do
the same thing in speaking, if you believe you can. Release
your body from its uncertainty and let it do what your
mind has taught it to do. Show the listener who is in
charge. Learn to think and act like a professional.

We know comparatively little about the human mind
and how it functions. But who really cares? We don't need
to know who dug the well or how deep the hole to
recognize that the water quenches our thirst.

From earliest youth, I searched for a truth
To guide me if I should digress.
Some magical ray to light up the way,

An arrow that points down the road to success.

Each fad that I found and followed around
In search of this mythical scheme,
Failed every test and dissolved like the rest,
A useless, discarded, impractical dream.

At last it was clear I'd never been near
To the secret I struggled to find.
For the method I sought must rise up from thought;
It's a strange, magic power that flows from my mind.

—Will Turner

Assuming that you have prepared the speech and are ready to go on, following are a few hints to help you in the prespeaking period:

1. Pick appropriate clothes and say, "These are my best. They look right, and I'm very comfortable." Get expert help if you think you need it.

2. Fix your hair the way you want it, and *then forget about it.*

3. Practice your speech and your voice exercises during the times set aside for such things and forget them in the moments before you speak, except for the warm-up exercises described in Chapter 6.

4. Believe in what you are saying. Direct your attention outside yourself.

Now assure yourself that there is nothing more you can do. You are ready. You are complete. You are competent.

People often ask me, "But what should I do just before I speak? Should I walk? Should I visit with people? What's best?" Individual preferences and personal differences provide the answers to these questions. Generalization is impossible. Sometimes the decision is made for us by the circumstances of the occasion. At a banquet, for example, you are usually expected to sit at the head table. At a meeting, you must often be near the platform or readily accessible to it. Whenever possible, I like to walk, right up to the last minute. Usually I stroll alone in an isolated corridor or in the outdoors if it's possible. I seek a place where I can rehearse segments of my speech and visualize the performance. (But don't let people see you pacing. It gives a bad advance impression.) I avoid cocktail parties. I prefer not to visit with people at this time. On the other hand, some speakers divert their attention by purposely turning to others for conversation, and a few even seek the relaxing effect of one belt from across the bar. For myself, "no booze" is an inviolable rule. Alcohol tends to make me hoarse, and the voice is one of the most precious tools in the persuasion profession.

Visualize yourself speaking to an audience, to a customer, or even to your spouse. Conjure friendly faces looking at you. Imagine people laughing at your jokes, listening intently to your ideas, nodding agreement to the things you say. *In your mind you never have a failure.* Knowing this helps to reinforce success in a real situation.

> **SUCCESS SECRET: Think like a professional. Cast positive thoughts on the subconscious mind.**

And here is another way to compound your persuasive strength.

CAPTURE LIGHT FROM THE AFTERGLOW

There is a special way to reap the "compounding harvest." After every speech or conference presentation—even after important conversations—a period occurs in which the experience replays itself, flooding the brain with ideas. A remarkable clarity prevails. It is a time when you can recall everything you said. A voice inside seems to be dictating precisely how the performance could have been improved.

I always plan to capture this valuable moment. In a receptive mood, I usually sit with pad in hand and write down the impressions I receive:

1. How to improve organization.
2. Additional support items that suddenly reveal themselves.
3. Recollections of people and how they responded—when their attention lagged, when their faces lit up and their heads bobbed in agreement—and what I was saying at those moments.
4. What jokes and one-liners seemed to please my listeners, and which ones bombed.

As the onrush of these ideas begins to fade, I quickly revise my speech outline—deleting, adding, rearranging. The modifications are often minor, but always for the better. The process always assures me of two things:

1. My speech and conversation constantly improve under the critical light of listener responses.
2. My speech remains fresh for me. Stagnation from over-repetition never sets in.

NEVER GIVE UP

When you started to read this book and follow its directions, you embarked on a journey to excellence. I have watched scores of speakers reach that goal.

Do you remember Martha Jurgenson? She is the high-school student I invited to join our varsity speech team who later captured a national oratory championship. Martha never gave up. After school hours she came to my classroom for coaching. She volunteered to speak for community organizations. She learned to capture the light from the afterglow, and every speaking experience was better than the one before.

> **SUCCESS SECRET: You can learn quickly to be an excellent speaker, but the quest for superiority is a never-ending journey.**

Here is another impressive example of skill that derived from persistent practice:

I once addressed a Junior Chamber of Commerce group in a large city. That very evening the Jaycees launched a personal improvement project in public speaking. For one minute, each member was required to speak on the topic, "If I Were Mayor." If communication skill is a criterion for being mayor, that city was fortunate to have none of these young men as city leader.

Although aggressive in business, most of them suddenly became stammering adolescents behind the microphone. Voluntarily, a few came to me later for coaching. *All of them continued in the self-improvement program.* One year later, more by coincidence than on purpose, I returned to address the same group. I could hardly believe the transformation in these men. Not only were most of them very good, they were also *enjoying their speaking experiences.*

> **SUCCESS SECRET:** Thousands have climbed the ladder of success in speech and grasped the power of personal persuasion.

CLIMB ONWARD TO THE PINNACLE

I have presented the preceding examples, not because they are exceptions, but because *they are the rule.* What these people did, *you can do better!* As we draw near the end of the book, I repeat my words of constant encouragement: *Keep practicing the exercises I have given you.* I am sure you have tried them all, but time constraints obviously prevent you from repeating all of them every day. You can, however, select *one project to work on every day* so that your power of persuasion will continue to develop. The results you reap will compound with every effort you make.

Never turn aside from the opportunity to engage in relaxed, productive conversation. Listen to people. Toss response leads to them. Determine what needs to be said and watch how improvement flourishes in your interpersonal relations.

Create your own opportunities to speak. There is a process available so simple that you may have overlooked it. *Be a speech volunteer!* In large communities, the Chamber of Commerce often sponsors a speakers bureau. Register as a member. List your favorite and best topics. Accept a few assignments, then watch the invitations roll in.

Various service clubs are present in all communities, large and small. They offer a harvest of speaking opportunities. In jest we refer to this as the "knife-and-fork" circuit. You'll probably never be offered an honorarium, but there is a great, intangible reward called *experience*.

The church, the school, local trade associations, and many other groups are also fertile fields where you can plant your talent. These groups need programs; you need practice and exposure.

A few months before I wrote this chapter, a bright and bubbling college student majoring in business came to me to seek advice. She proclaimed her burning ambition to become a professional speaker.

"How do I start?" she asked. My responding advice was in seven stages:

1. Become an authority on subjects in which you have keen interest. Learn all there is to be known in those fields.
2. Build a speaker's file of magic gems: illustrations, quotations, humor, statistics.
3. Work on your self-image. Build self-confidence. Never deny your ability to reach your goal.
4. Learn the fundamentals of personal communication.
5. Converse with other people whenever you can. Never walk on the other side of the street to avoid contact.

6. Construct a twenty-minute speech. Practice it. Revise it. Make it ready for public exposure.

7. Volunteer for the "freebie" circuit. *Speak, speak, speak* whenever you can.

This young woman is currently working on her speech. When she is ready, I shall personally assist her to open doors that are outlets for her growing skills. But she doesn't really need me. Anyone can find those doors, open them, and fill the calendar with speaking engagements.

Most professional speakers started their careers on this pathway. It helped them to hone their skills. It enhanced their reputations so the *paid appearances naturally evolved.*

But the professional platform is probably not your goal. Small matter. The knife-and-fork circuit still offers a rich reward in magic development. In one year, before I turned to the professional microphone, I made more than fifty speeches to a broad cross-section of city organizations.

> **SUCCESS SECRET:** Graduate as soon as possible from "facing the mirror" to holding the attention of a real, live audience.

PRESS THE MAGIC-MEMORY STAMP

We have nearly reached the end of our flight. To summarize the ground we have covered, mile by mile, is virtually impossible. But I do want to make passing mention of the *main things you should be attaining.*

1. Your attitude towards yourself is a primary matter. I am convinced that self-acceptance is the first requirement for success in nearly all endeavors, and particularly in speech and conversation. I have also discovered that doubting one's self-worth is a gnawing enemy of an enor-

mous part of our nation's population. *Always appraise yourself highly.* Drop the words "I can't" from your vocabulary. It may be true that "no one is perfect," but don't be forever obsessed with your imperfections or let them be an eternal barrier to your success.

> **SUCCESS SECRET: One of the great rewards of persuasive speaking is a changed attitude toward oneself.**

2. Your voice is an indispensable tool of persuasive speaking. It has the power to move people—to excite them, to quiet them, to influence them. You may never acquire the mellow tones of a movie idol, but you *can sound pleasant.* You can gracefully manipulate variables—pitch, rate and volume—to generate your magic power.

3. Your body, too, is a potent instrument of persuasion. The arms, the head, the face—even the feet—contribute to the communication process. Have you ever noticed how a waitress may proceed to fill your coffee cup, even when you clearly state you have had enough? Next time, don't tell her; instead, extend your hand, palm down, near your cup and wave your hand back and forth laterally at the wrist. Never will a drop of coffee leave the waitress's pot. Study body language from the actions of little kids to the gestures of professional communicators. Practice doing what they do, and you will strengthen your persuasive power.

4. Words are symbols of our thoughts. Without words thought could not exist, and for the most part communication would degenerate into imprecision. *Words carry meaning and emotion.* Effective speakers blend dynamic words into persuasive sentences. Constantly add new and usable words to your vocabulary, simple words whose vowels are packed with punch. Let your listeners hear the noise of *smack* and *crash.* Let them feel the softness of *smooth* and *hush* and *calm.* Practice varying the length, arrangement,

and rhythm of your sentences. Read good speeches from the mouths and pens of the experts. Don't *borrow* their works, but *emulate* them, using language tools that conjure specific, concrete images in your listener's mind.

5. In this final magic-memory stamp, I shall group the three traditional divisions of the speech: the *opening*, the *body*, and the *closing*. Earlier in the book each was given a separate chapter, but in reality they form a unity, a harmonious whole. At the beginning of your speech—a critical moment—select a strong device for penetrating the audience barrier; then proceed through the persuasive process, constantly reaching out to touch your audience with magnetic material. Learn to speak without notes, but if notes are needed, even if you must use a full script, remember that persuasive power is yours only if there is a chemical blend between you and your listeners. *Capture them. Drive your message home.* Carefully plan the closing of your speech; never leave the landing to chance or merely "feel" your way to the landing strip. Use one of the many techniques available that will add a power-packed climax to your message.

6. No speech can ever reach maximum power unless it is well-laced with quotations and illustrations. Humor can also lend a hand. Your speech file of magic gems and humorous stories is one of your best friends. In your reading, your conversation, and your day-to-day experiences, be alert for material that will increase the power you need. Record items as soon as you find them. Unless you write them down, they will quickly disappear into the quicksand of your mind, never to reappear.

7. You may be called on from time to time to perform special assignments: introduce a speaker, lead a discussion, answer questions from the audience, or make a spontaneous speech. Learn the format for these tasks, and you will be able to do them with poise and confidence even on the spur of the moment.

8. Visual aids are often a strong kind of support for your presentation, but they must be used correctly. Nothing is more distracting or more destructive than visual props that are poorly planned and badly constructed. Learn the rules. Practice integrating your slides, chart boards, and transparencies into the total presentation. If properly used, visual aids add strong support to your persuasion.

LET PERSUASIVE POWER GROW WITHIN YOU

The road to excellence converges as a tiny dot on the faraway horizon. Don't become discouraged when I say that you will never reach it, for as you approach that dot, it moves steadily onward toward a more distant horizon. One never reaches it because there are always new speeches, new audiences, and new occasions to conquer.

But, as you *do* approach each of these horizons you discover a progressive growth in your magic power. Your confidence soars after each successful experience, and your performance level rises as well. Whenever you deliver a new speech or face a new audience in a fresh environment, you will find yourself concentrating on the psychology of persuasion—on substance. No longer will you be distracted by the mechanical details of body, voice, or even sentence structure. These elements have now become natural, spontaneous parts of your new-found power. They are accomplished without effort and they are performed without conscious thought. Such is the itinerary of the dedicated person who sincerely strives for persuasive power.

You have now fulfilled the "law of attainment." It has three parts:

1. Learn
2. Practice
3. Improve

Continue on the road you are traveling. Practice your way to excellence. Move onward to become a new person— a new you—who knows the *secrets of personal persuasion.*

Index